Love to Change? Then Change to Love

Heart Art 'Magic'
By Marian Egan

Co. Kildare 2011

Copyright © 2011 Marian Egan

© 2011 by *Marian Egan*

All rights reserved.

All Rights Reserved. No part of this publication may be reproduced in any form or by any means, including scanning, photocopying, or otherwise without prior written permission of the copyright holder.

Disclaimer and Terms of Use: The Author and Publisher has strived to be as accurate and complete as possible in the creation of this book, notwithstanding the fact that he does not warrant or represent at any time that the contents within are accurate due to the rapidly changing nature of the Internet. While all attempts have been made to verify information provided in this publication, the Author and Publisher assumes no responsibility for errors, omissions, or contrary interpretation of the subject matter herein. Any perceived slights of specific persons, peoples, or organizations are unintentional. In practical advice books, like anything else in life, there are no guarantees of income made. Readers are cautioned to reply on their own judgment about their individual circumstances to act accordingly. This book is not intended for use as a source of legal, business, accounting or financial advice. All readers are advised to seek services of competent professionals in legal, business, accounting, and finance field.

First Printing, 2011

Printed in the United States of America

Dedicated to my mother Phyllis Kane

and

In Loving Memory of my brother Tony aged 3. Because of his loss my destiny was transformed. It has made me into the person I am today. I will always be grateful for the lessons I learnt as a result of his passing

I especially dedicate this book to my husband Damien who continually gave his unconditional love, support and encouragement, every day to help me stay positive and upbeat while I was going through my Journey to Success

Love to Change? Then Change to Love

Creating your
'Breakthrough to Freedom and Success'

By Marian Egan

Table of Contents

Introduction 9
The Beginning of the End!!! 11
Painting of 'New Life' 14
Photograph of ' New Life' 15
Chapter 1 - My story 16
Chapter 2 - Another Knock in Life 20
Chapter 3 – Another Life threatening event 22
Chapter 4 - Here I go again! 25
Chapter 5 - At the end of 2005 I was involved in a car crash 28
Chapter 6 - My Heart Art 'Magic' Journey 30
Chapter 7 - What Is Heart Art "Magic" 32
Chapter 8 - How Heart Art Helped Me to Make Changes 34
Paintings Flow Explained 36
Meditation & Centering 37
Inspirational Daily Living 38
Circle of Life 40
Hands of Light 42
Rainbow Sunset 44
Flight of Freedom 46
Centre of Empowerment 48
Forest of Anger 50
In the Midst 52
Painful Separation – In FULL Separation 54
Elementary Sanctuary 56
Spiritual Flow 58
Chain Reaction 60

Vibration of life	62
Head above Water	64
Camouflage	66
Growth in Motion	68
The Big Bang	70
Peaceful Strength	72
Flight of Strength	74
Emergence	76
Vision Circles	78
Seeds of Life	80
Missing Links	82
Face your Fear	84
Paradise Retreat	86
Transformation	88
Olympic Torch - Lighting my Way	90
Nurturer of Nature – Giving Strength, Grace and Agility	92
Yipee De Do Da!!! – Celebration of Life's Freedom	94
Depths of Being - Where I can feed myself spiritually	96
In the Distance – Enjoy being still in the present (Now = Won)	98
Trilogy – At one with Heart and Mind = Unity of Self	100
Gut Feeling	102
Into the Core	104
Wisdom in Balance	106
Reflection	108
Growing and Knowing	110
Watching Movements	112
Keeping Tranquility	114
Life Flow – Being sure that you know	116
Creative Explosion	118
Flowing & Growing	120
'Five Elements' Strength in Stillness	122
Protected invitation to the Light	124
Life Force Vortex	126

Come into the Light	128
Let's Party	130
"Out of" or "Into" – I choose	132
"Busy Busy Busy" – Take time out	134
Ready Steady Go – Have Some Fun	136
"Secret Hideaway" – Escape When I Need To	138
Cellular Activity – Creating what I want at primary level	140
Let's Play	142
Follow your Dream	144
Peaceful Place	146
Flower Power	148
Into The Stillness	150
Creative Explosions	152
At Ease	154
Coming Home	156
Golden Growth Inspiration	158
Rainbow Dance	160
Sea Heaven	162
Reflective Peace:	164
Midday Flight	166
Gathering Focus	168
Relaxing Tranquility	170
Out on a Limb	172
Protectors of my Inner Child	174
Softened Heart in Motion	176
Lighthearted gift to myself	178
Birthing of Past Fears	180
"Time" to flow into Stillness (stem the flow)	182
Heart Centre – Staying Calm & Focused	184
Relax, Have Fun & Play	186
Twilight Forest	188
Fireworks – Letting Go	190
Floral Gift	192
Balanced Chakra Flow – Mind Body Spirit	194
Releasing the Transformation	196
Doorway to Freedom – light, love, harmony & contentment	198

Final Separation 200
Flight, Cunning, Wisdom, Strength, Lightness 202
Walkway 204
Dialogue Nomed & ME 206
Smiles & Styles 208
Bird Of Paradise 210
Underwater Tranquility – Going with the Flow
.... 212
Transcend into Calmness 214
Forgiveness for Freedom 216
Fearless – Freedom from Fear 218
A Love Heart Gift to Myself 220
Rock Steady Balance – A Cut Thru – Break-Thru
.... 222
Blue Haven 224
Extraction 226
Filling the Void 228
Another start 230
Birthing 232
New Beginnings - A wiser head on young shoulders 234
Time for Play 236
Calling IN 238
Imbalance – Keep Balance Always 240
Connection is Key 242

Chapter Nine – The door to freedom 244

How to get started using Heart Art 'Magic' painting process. 248
Relaxation / Meditation 250

Conclusion 251
About the Author 254
Addendum - My Juice Plus + ® story 255

Introduction

"Are we lost"? The six your old said. I replied, "No, we are not lost, we are here, we just do not know where here is". We were in Paris, with very little time to spare before we were to board the TGV for the south of France, and we had come up from the metro to see if we could bring the children to get a quick glimpse of the Eifel Tower. We were not even close to the area, so we abandoned the idea. Did you ever feel lost inside yourself and could not understand why?

In reflection, my life was like that from a very young age. I was lost and traumatised. But, I did not have a clue what was happening. I spent my life looking for contentment and peace outside of myself, but never found it there. From the age of eight, there was a void inside myself that I was trying to fill, which was created in 1963 and was finally filled in Nov 2010.

The contents of this book and this way of working eventually helped me to fill this void and made me feel whole again. For me, this was an extreme length of time which I had invested in making this discovery. This is the reason I am willing to share my painful experience, so that I can possibly help someone else to find a quicker, easier and effective solution to their problems.

The realizations that I made during my time of working with Heart Art 'Magic', was truly magic. It helped me reach depths, deep down within myself that I did not know existed until I saw my paintings reveal their meaning to me, and some of them even brought me to my knees. I had no idea that I could be the instigator of feeling peace, happiness, contentment, tranquility and the most amazing positive qualities that I had been missing for most of my life.

I discovered these qualities were always there within me, but because I had lived my life in 'fear' and dread, at a 'very deep' level that I seldom got to nurture them. They had been buried for so long and I had been unable to reach them to let them rise to the surface.

Don't get me wrong, I had wonderful happy times during my lifetime, with my husband, my family and friends. And I was so fortunate to have lived the life I have. There was this 'missing link' though, and I did not know what it was. It took me a very long time to realise that it was 'my relationship with myself'; I tortured myself every day, at a subconscious level. I was not aware of what I was doing or why I was doing it. If I knew how this 'episode' was going to affect me I would have done what I could to prevent it. But when it was not in my consciousness, I was totally 'unaware', so I couldn't deal with it.

As a result of my feelings, I did not like myself, and I especially did not love myself. I could not understand how anyone could love me or even like me. How could they do that? How could anyone have any nice feelings towards me in any way, shape or form, when I could not embrace these feelings for myself?

Over the years, I found that for me to change, I needed to change. The first thing I had to do was so huge but yet so simple, I needed to love myself. It was only in doing this that I could make this breakthrough. How could this one little thing 'loving myself' make such a difference in my life and enable me to make 'massive' changes' within me.

Heart Art 'Magic' facilitated this empowerment and showed me what I needed to 'see' so that I could make the change. It helped me 'breakthrough to freedom and success'. I am so grateful for this experience.

The Beginning of the End!!!

"Damien, what will I use as a book cover, I have no idea what it needs to be"? I asked. "Why don't you take some time out and sit in silence, see what ideas come to mind and then paint what you feel." Damien replied. Now why didn't I think of that? I have always painted how I was feeling but never thought to do it for direction. What a great idea!

I took myself into in my studio, lit a candle and sat in silence for a while and waited for inspiration to come. I honestly didn't feel (at the time) that I was getting any vibes except I knew and could see the colours that I wanted to choose. After ten minutes or so, I started with that concept and chose purple, red and turquoise. I took my pot of wallpaper paste and covered the background with the past, dipped my hands in the colours and spread the paint on the paper, working them together going around and around. I was really enjoying the feeling of the paint mixing and blending together. With the movements I had created, I could see the heart shape appear.

I filled this in with the red paint and once again applied it with my hands. I wanted to use a very thick layer of red, which I did. I was happy with how it looked, but more importantly I realy enjoyed the whole process of the painting.

As always, when I paint, I got the camera and took a photo as soon as I was finished. I was pleased with how it went and it felt good, but I was not really overjoyed about the outcome of the painting. Okay, it was a heart shape which would represent the concept of the book, but it didn't have the wow factor that I felt would make a good front cover for this book.

I came back to the house and told Damien I had completed it and he asked "how did it go"? I told him of my experience and asked him to come and look at the finished painting; it was still drying in the studio.

He was busy with his own project at this time, and said he would come out as soon as he could. So I took the camera to show him the photograph instead. When I looked at the '**photograph of the painting**' I could not believe what I was seeing. The photograph is the painting on the front cover. There is no yellow or orange in the painting itself.

I had to go back into my studio to look at the finished painting to compare it to what was captured in the' photograph'. It looks like two different paintings, one with just the red heart and the photograph also has the red heart but it also has a life of its own, with the vibrant yellow right in the centre of this heart shape. Damien thought I had done two different paintings.

To me, it looks as if there is a 'new life' growing in the centre of the heart, shining brightly in yellow, with a vibrant yellow white light shining down on it from above. Look at the painting 'New Life' on page 14 and compare it to the '**photograpgh of the painting**' on page 15. I am amazed at what has transpired. I asked for direction for the 'book cover', I took the time to sit in silence and waited until I was ready to paint, and I went with the flow of what I was feeling. The result that I was given was more than I had asked for.

I am blown away by what has been presented to me in this painting, and it has given me a new strength in believing and trusting the guidance I can tap into. Being in the 'present moment' and tapping into my own 'Source' brought about the most wonderful 'transformation' in the photograph. Showing me something that 'is there' but 'not there' or 'not visible' to the naked eye.

Just because we cannot see something, it does not mean that it is not there. We have so much energy that we can draw on. Remembering to do it every day and connecting to this direction can help us to reach our full potential in life. I am inspired and directed to share my journey in this format, but even more so after the 'Magical' revelation of the front cover.

Chapter 1 - My story

To fully appreciate the power of this book I need to start at the beginning. My life changed when I was eight years old. I really do not remember much of my childhood before this time, but I began living my nightmare from the age of eight in May 1963. There were two incidents that happened within eight weeks of each other that changed me forever. I was shocked and traumatized by the first incident, but the second one stole the essence of my being.

I was out playing one afternoon near my house with my two 'best friends' Mary and Robin, (names changed). Mary and I used to regularly fight over which one of us was going to marry Robin when we grew up. We both loved him dearly and we enjoyed playing together. The three of us were inseparable. We were happily playing this day when Robin was accidently knocked down by a bus a few yards from his house. We had been playing together. It was horrific to see him lying by the bus on the roadside. I cannot remember if he died there and then or later that day in the hospital. His mother and family were devastated. He was their only son and he was the youngest in his family.

My mother and Robin's mother were great friends. They saw each other every day. My mom comforted Robin's mom and did all she could as any neighbour would do, to help her get over her loss. Mary and I were inconsolable. We had each other, but we missed Robin every day. I lived in an area where there were three bus routes that passed by my house several times a day. My mom had warned us to be extremely careful when we were out and about. We were reminded to stay safe and to watch out for each other.

The next accident changed my life forever and made me the person I am today. It was too much to bear at any time, but especially as it came so soon after Robin's death. This dreadful day began on a summer's afternoon when I was out playing with a group of friends that lived across the road from me. Mary was not with me this day.

I was also minding my younger brother Tony at the time. I usually minded Tony for mom. Mom was expecting another baby and was heavily pregnant, and I loved minding Tony. He was just 3 years old. Blond curly hair and blue eyed. He was a little angel. It was time for Tony to go home and have his tea. So Mom came out into the side garden and called me to bring him across the road. I was in the middle of a game and was just about to stop playing so that I could bring him over to mom when my friend said "you stay and finish, I am out of the game, I will bring him across the road for you".

She took Tony by the hand and was about to bring him across to mom. I heard mom shouting over to us to "hold tightly on to Tony", because there was a bus coming around the corner. I remember saying to myself. "She is not used to toddlers" so I jumped up and was rushing out the gate to grab hold of his hand. Tony spotted mom, and as soon as he did he pulled away from my friend and ran across the road, and went straight under the bus. I watched in horror. I could not believe that this had just happened. Not again. "Please God, not again". Not to Tony. He was so tiny and fragile. He was still a baby. It could NOT be happening.

I can still see it now, in slow motion, and it is as fresh today in my mind as it was that dreadful day. I remember kneeling over him and thinking that he was okay, because there wasn't a mark on him. He just lay there motionless. The rest is a blur. I do not remember the following sequence of events. Except for later, when my dad got home from work, and he was told what had happened, he raced out to his car to get to the hospital. Tony died that day. And I blamed myself for what happened to him. It was my fault, because I did not mind him and I did not keep him safe.

I did not mind him well enough. If only I had brought him out the gate myself, he would still have tried to run across the road, but my grip on him would have been vice-like, and he would not have got away from me. My friend was not used to toddlers and as soon as Tony saw my mom, he easily pulled away from her. I didn't usually play in their garden. In fact, they would come and play in our garden as it was bigger.

My parents never blamed me for what happened that day. They didn't need to. I did that all by myself, and from then on I lived in shame, guilt, and blame. That day changed my life. I functioned from then on. I existed, and tried to stay out of other people's way, including my family. I would hide away on my own as much as I could. We lived in a three bedroom semi detached house. There was nowhere to hide except the attic. I would climb up there and spend as much time on my own.

I loved making things and I loved knitting. I spent many hours hidden away there. I would wait until no one was watching before I would lift the hatch and climb up on the door and into the attic space. There was no room to stand up. I could only crouch down and sit. Luckily dad had installed a light in the attic and I could see what I was doing. This was my refuge and I knit and knit, it helped to stop me feeling. It helped me to be creative and I felt as though I was doing something useful..

The day after Tony died my sister and I was sent away to relatives for a week while the funeral took place, and we came home to an empty house. There was no sign of Tony ever have been there. His shoes were gone and his clothes were all gone as well. It was like he had never existed. The pain of his departure was growing every day in me and for the rest of the family.

I do not know how my parents got through this painful time. I must have been horrendous. It was so hard for me and my brothers and sisters, what must it have been like for my parents? My mom cried all the time and sometimes I could hear her wailing at night when she was supposed to be sleeping. When she cried, I cried. It never got any easier. As I grew up, it became harder to bear. I was dying inside and I didn't know how to make the pain stop. It got worse and worse. My ability to function lessened and I felt extremely low as I tried to suppress my feelings of grief and guilt.

I can remember mom bringing me to see doctor after doctor to find out what was wrong with me, I had no energy. I was prescribed lotions and potions to build myself up. At one point mom was told to cut my hair, as the doctor thought that most of my energy was going into growing it long. The real crux of the matter was the feelings of guilt, blame and shame. I continued to suppress these feelings and bury them as deep as I could, to try to keep them hidden.. I didn't know how to handle them; in fact I didn't know what they were.

I know now that I was extremely depressed. I did not want to go to school, go outside to play, or socialise in any way. When I did go out, I made sure that I pulled the hood of my coat up so that nobody would notice me as I walked down the road. I felt that everyone could see the 'shame' that I felt. It was as though I had 'guilt' written across my forehead.

I only spoke to people if they addressed me first. I never initiated conversations. I was embarrassed to be seen in public. When I think of the punishment I brought upon myself at that time, I feel, now as an adult, that I was very hard on myself.

But, as a child, I always did as I was told and enjoyed being obedient. It was my nature. To me, on the day that Tony died, I didn't do as I was told and bring him home safely. I felt that I had done the worst possible thing in my life and I suffered the consequences. I felt as though I had killed him myself by my actions, or inaction as it turned out.

Chapter 2 - Another Knock in Life

I was living my life in fear and I was drowning in sorrow for the loss of my brother, then one day, at the age of twelve I was knocked down by a car as I crossed the road. I remember I was going to the cinema with my best friend Mary. It was a Sunday afternoon. That is all I remember until I woke up in the hospital. My parents were there in the hospital with me, but I didn't know who they were at the time as. I was so confused. I didn't know where I was, who I was, or why I was lying in bed with the biggest headache I had ever experienced, and these strangers talking to me and asking weird questions.

I remember opening my eyes and they asked me question after question about what had happened and I didn't know what they were talking about. I could not answer them anyway. I just wanted to drift away and sleep. When I woke again I was on my own, I think it was the next day. My mother told me later when I had recovered, that when she heard I was knocked down, she thought that she had lost me, as well as having lost Tony.

I spent a week in the hospital. I had minor cuts, bruises and stitches in my arm and head, but the bang I received on my head was the worst injury. To this day, I have no memory of what happened. As well as the amnesia, this episode left me with severe migraine headaches. It was a very confusing time for me.

It was great to get home, but it was really challenging as well. Getting to know the family and fitting back into family life was another struggle. I don't think I ever fit back in fully within the family unit because at this stage I know I had withdrawn into myself, much deeper that before.

When I had time to think of what had happened to me I felt that I got what I deserved, it was justice, because I did not mind Tony and he died as a result of my negligence. I had taken a very negative mindset on board, and I felt that I may as well have 'killed' Tony myself. I never saw his death as an accident. I focused on him dying because I did not do what I was told. Had I taken his hand that day, none of this would have happened. Therefore, it was my entire fault.

One of the hardest things I found was going back into school after my accident, I could not remember names. And as for the academic side of school, it slipped back even further than it had before. I felt really isolated and alone and totally scared. I was living in fear. I found it was more difficult to remember subjects, and I was useless at homework. I dreaded getting up in the morning and going to school every day. I hated Mondays as I felt it was the start of another week of torture and I loved Fridays as I could get away from the pressure of going to school.

Chapter 3 – Another Life threatening event

The second time I was knocked down by a car was at the age of thirty five. This was another big blow to my body and mind, but it was also a turning point for me. I went out to cycle to the shops one day and came across a neighbour who was also going my way. I walked with her and congratulated her on the arrival of her second baby who was a few days old. She had her first son with her who was aged three, blond curly hair and beautiful big brown eyes.

We talked as we walked and caught up on how the new baby was settling in at home. We were nearing the shops when I saw this car coming speeding straight towards us. Before my brain registered what was happening, the driver ploughed into us and knocked us down. I had no time to react, it happened so fast. He hit the two of us full on and missed the toddler. The reason being, the toddler was straggling behind his mom even though she had a hold of his hand. When I could, I got up and went to pick the toddler up off the road. He was hysterical and his mom was badly injured with a broken leg and shoulder.

She was confused and kept asking me over and over again what had happened.. We were taken to the hospital by ambulance and I was allowed home later that night. I had a few cuts and many bruises but nothing broken, except my spirit. I came home from the hospital with my neighbours' husband who asked me to ring the maternity hospital and ask the ward sister to re-admit the new baby. The baby had only come home the day before. We collected the newborn baby and brought him back into Dublin to be re-admitted so that he would be taken care of. I did this, but I found it hard to do. I felt I should mind him myself, but I physically was unable.

It was extremely late in the evening by the time I got home to see my own family and for them to see me. My husband Damien was really concerned as we had not been able to speak directly with each other until then. As I told him what had happened, my body started to go into shock and I could not stop shaking, and then the tears started and I totally lost my control and my composure. I had held myself together all that day because I felt I had too.

It was a horrible experience, but yet it brought me down so much physically and mentally I was totally unable to handle what had happened. I feel that this was a total breakdown or as I always say now in hindsight, a total 'breakthrough' and the only way I could go now, was back up.

I remember standing at the sink one day soon after this incident. I was preparing vegetables for the dinner that evening, when I started to feel this eruption happening in my body. I felt as if something was 'bursting' to come up my throat and out my mouth. I felt as though I can no longer control my emotions, they were ready to explode, and I could no longer suppress them anymore. I had to seek professional help.

I was referred to a specialist and ended up on medication to get me through this period which lasted a few years. This helped me cope at the time, but it did not address the cause of **_why_** my body and especially my mind reacted to this situation. I realised that the lesson for me was; I could relate to the three year old being knocked down with me, to the day that Tony was killed back in 1968. I re-lived that day over and over, again and again.

There is only so much tension that our body can take and when it has exceeded that tension, an explosion can happen. Think of it as a pressure cooker, it can blow, when the pressure becomes too much. As the eight year old back in 1968, I had learnt to suppress the pain, grief, guilt and hurt, so deep down within me, they were 'locked in' and this recent road accident could no longer contain these painful emotions that I had buried back then. They had 'surfaced' and I had to face them.

This episode finally broke my spirit. I could not function on a daily basis. The Demon had surfaced and I could not contain it any longer. It was out, I felt broken but I had to do something to help me through this time. I had my own family now to take care of. They knew nothing of my past or how it was affecting me now. I certainly do not know how Damien coped with me during this time. He has been so supportive in every way. I cried oceans. The tears were endless. I was crying as the adult who was hurting physically and mentally and as the eight year old who carried this 'secret' for a lifetime.

This was a turning point for me, although I did not know it. At that time, I thought my world had come to an end, yet it was only the beginning. The beginning of a healing process that could have happened earlier in life, but didn't. I thought that I would never, ever feel 'right' again. It took more than a year, possibly nearer two years to go through this part of my healing.

I went with the medication that I was prescribed, and it got me through this period of my life. The medication was necessary and it worked on my *symptoms* but unfortunately it did not address the *cause* of my **PROBLEM.**

Chapter 4 - Here I go again!

In 2000 I woke up on January 5th, I knew I was in trouble when I realised I could not get out of bed. I struggled with the question of why is this happening to me. I had a problem with my spine and found walking a challenge. I had never experienced pain like this before. I felt imobilised. I cancelled my appointments for my clients in my clinic and rescheduled them for the following week. I spent the week in bed, but at the end of the week I still could not walk properly or stand up for any length of time, so I had to re set my appointments for the next week. This problem continued to persist. Weeks later I was still no better, so I cancelled my appointments for my clients for the foreseeable future. I had no idea what was happening and I was in extreme pain. I spent the next four months in bed. My children and Damien took on the job of taking care of me and taking care of the house and all that it entailed. It was a very challenging time for me and equally hard on all my family. I was experiencing severe pain even when I was lying flat out in bed.

I spent the time listening to personal development tapes, and reading inspirational and tutorial books to help me to get through my day. I called it my 'University of Life' and I feel I did a Masters Degree in 'Life Lessons'. We are human beings, not human doings. I learnt how to '**be**'. I felt I spent this TIMEOUT wisely and I received a lot out of it. Physically it was very painful. Emotionally and mentally I found this timeout extremely difficult and it was four months before I could get about with crutches.

By the time June came around I had progressed from two crutches to one crutch and eventually I managed to walk unaided. I thought that I was doing really well, and I was, until something fell on the floor and I realised that there was no way I could bend down to pick it up. I was unable to function to do everyday things around the house. When I went back to the hospital in June, my doctor wanted to send me for a second opinion, and he asked me to go and see a neurosurgeon. I agreed but I was wondering how long it would take to get an appointment with a neurosurgeon. My doctor went into the next room to make a phone call to see what he could arrange. He came back into his office and told me he had arranged an appointment the very next day, which was a Thursday. I had to go to Beaumont hospital in Dublin for this appointment.

On the Friday morning I was admitted as an emergency case to have surgery on my spine. I had no time to think, it was a whirlwind of change in such a short space of time. I was so tired of the constant pain that I didn't care anymore. Surgery was not a route that I had wanted to take. I had resisted it from the start. But now I was presented with it, I decided to go ahead. I needed to get back to normality.

My recovery took some time. After a while I realised that the mechanics of my back was better and I could pick things up from the floor, but I had no energy. I was unable to function properly and do everyday tasks, and I found standing and sitting was still a problem. The only comfort I got was when I was lying down. I began taking the best quality vitamins and minerals every day, to boost my immune system, but they made no difference. I may as well have eaten sweets.

This lack of energy and pain went on for another two years. I was so frustrated and desperate at this time, that I was beginning to wonder would I ever get my life back to normal. I wanted to get back to teaching exercise and fitness classes, plus go back to running my clinic. I also wanted to enjoy my life, and my family and by now my grandchild Amy was born. I was missing out on so much. Then I experienced another ***turning point*** in my life.

Turning Point

This time it was a wonderful introduction that would literally change my life and restore my physical health. In September 2002 I was introduced to **Juice Plus+®** whole food nutrition which eventually gave me back my health. It is not a quick fix, and it is not a cure for any illness. But for me, it was a long term solution. I started taking **Juice Plus+®** and it was the best decision I could have made. Physically, I was better than ever and was able to go back to teaching fitness classes and I re-opened my clinical practice and went back to work. I was fascinated that something so simple and so natural could make such a difference to my life. I had almost given up hope of ever making a full recovery. I owe my gratitude to Mr. Damian Brennan, who took the time to meet me and invite me to hear about **Juice Plus+®.**

Natural wholefood nutrition takes time to work. Just as the seasons take time to come and go, the natural essence of the powders in **Juice Plus+®** capsules also requires the same length of time. For the next three years I was doing great and life was really good, until!

Chapter 5 - At the end of 2005 I was involved in a car crash

I was going with my daughter into Dublin on the day a car crashed into the back of mine. I was stopped at traffic lights when this happened. The jolt I got from the impact was horrendous. I was turned in my seat while I was speaking to Stephanie. I didn't realise that this incident would upset my back again and I found myself in the same painful situation as before. It meant a return to the hospital, more doctors and surgeon appointments, and yet again I was unable to work. I was imobilised for another long spell. Walking and standing once again was a problem. I couldn't work. I was no longer a functioning wife, mother, washer upper, cooker, cleaner, shopper or therapist. I was beginning to have the 'why me' attitude. But I knew that this was only going to make matters worse and would not serve me well at all. Negativity invites negativity. Positive thoughts invites positive energy where I can make changes.

I returned to my 'University of Life' (in my bed) and started another 'Master's Degree'. I did not know how I would come out of it this time. Would I pass or would I 'give in' and become a victim once more. My family stepped up to the mark again and took care of me throughout this time. But this episode was a longer 'timeout' than before. This was another **big** step on my Life Ladder. This step had to be going upwards for me or otherwise I was going down. I could not afford that 'direction' again. I had spent my most of my life 'existing' there. I realised that once again, it was up to me to make the right choice on the outcome of this situation. To fuel my body I had to get my 'thinking right' I had to keep it right.

I persevered through 2006 having one therapy after another to help ease the pain. Finally under the guidance of the neurosurgeon I had another spinal operation in March of 2007 which did not go well. My recovery was slower this time and walking was harder than it had been before. I had more time on my hands, and once again I used this time wisely and as best I could. During this period of my 'timeout' I was able to help other people with their health by introducing them to **Juice Plus+®**. I had the phone and my virtual office, and that was all I needed so that I could run my **Juice Plus+®** business from my bed. This also helped with my where I was at. It helped to keep me upbeat most times, although there were times when I was screaming inside. It was difficult to hide my emotions. My family was the only ones to witness the really hard episodes I experienced.

I decided that I was never having surgery again as it had not solved my problem. Having consulted with the neurosurgeon during 2007 and having more tests and scans, my sciatic nerve was now trapped and this was why I could not make a full stride when I tried to walk. During 2006 and 2007, it was extremely challenging; I was unable to work in my clinic. I had difficulty walking and standing was a major problem. I was really frustrated at what was happening. I was still reading my tutorial and inspirational books, which helped me to stay sane.

My physical state had become so bad at the end of 2007 and early 2008 that I decided I could no longer carry on as I was .I was a prisoner in my body and in my house. I was no longer independent. The pain was too much at times and the restriction was unbearable. I had had enough and needed more medical intervention. I was admitted to hospital for more surgery in March 2008 where I had another spinal surgery procedure.

Chapter 6 - My Heart Art 'Magic' Journey

It was unfortunate that I experienced tragedy at such a young age of eight. I did not know how to handle the outcome or the grief, and I internalized it at that time, because I did not understand what was happening, and I was too young to know what to do.

It has taken me a very long time, nearly my whole lifetime, to realise that the painful loss I suffered was self-inflicted; I had blamed myself for so long. I felt that I had lived through a life sentence. What was really instrumental in bringing my life 'full circle' and healing the grief, the hurt, the blame and shame was my experience with paint, and the Heart Art 'Magic' workshops I went to. My wonderful mentor Marie Perret is an English lady who lives in France. She came to Ireland to facilitate these Heart Art 'Magic' workshops.

"When your eyes see your hands do the work of your heart, your circle of life is complete"

My Heart Art 'Magic' journey began in December 2006. I am so grateful for having been given the opportunity to experience this. It has opened up an outlet for the most wonderful change to happen within me, which was a beautiful and gentle but very effective and efficient way of healing. It helped me to deal with the physical pain I was in. It also enabled me to deal with the emotional pain as well. Most importantly, it showed me where the mental pain was coming from. Heart Art 'Magic' helped ***dissolve*** all of this pain as it showed me, what I needed to look at, why I needed to see it, and finally the process of 'letting go' of the pain, this happened as I progressed through my Heart Art 'Magic' journey.

I am so grateful to have experienced this 'gift of healing' that I want to share it with anyone who ever suffered pain in their life. Whether it 'was' or 'is' physical pain, emotional or mental pain. At some point in everyone's life there are painful episodes. Some experience pain for short stages, others experience pain that can go on for many years. Mine went on for far too long, and it did not need to. I did not know that at the time. I could have dealt with it differently, if I had of known how. I now have the answer. 'How' to deal with pain, 'ease' the pain and finally 'release' the pain. This is what I want to share with you.

This book can give you an insight to the healing process that we all have within us and can access when we have the knowledge and understanding of how to do this. I have also included in this book the painting process and the paintings that I would like to share with you so that you can also 'see' my progression and have an understanding of how Heart Art 'Magic' works.

M – My

A – Ability to

G – Go

I – Into my

C – Centre

Meditation is the magic. Painting is the process for expression. Then, taking the time to 'sit with the outcome' (paintings) and write about how you felt while you were painting and what these paintings are showing you. This is the Heart Art 'Magic' process of healing, which can unlock your full potential, to be the best that you can be in your lifetime.

Heart Art 'Magic' can help to take your mind off of the pain. You become so engrossed in the process of the painting that it can give you a 'break away' from the constant indicator that something is not 'right' (pain) in your Brain/Body.

Chapter 7 - What Is Heart Art "Magic"

Heart Art 'Magic' is spontaneous painting. Or painting from your heart, without THINKING what the outcome will be. You paint what you FEEL. What I mean by that is, taking the time to sit and be still, do nothing, say nothing, think nothing. It might help initially if you listen to soothing music to get you into a state of total relaxation before you paint. Also concentrating on your breathing can bring you into a meditative state. It is the stillness that starts the process of this way of painting. Heart Art 'Magic' is ***ALL*** about the **process** and very little to do with the outcome, or finished painting.

The picture that is produced is not as important as 'how you FEEL' while you are painting it. Obviously the painting has a story to tell and it is wonderful figuring this out at the end of a session. Sometimes you know instantly, what message the painting is giving you. Then there are times that you need to reflect on the finished painting before the message is revealed. It is so exciting and rewarding but more importantly it can work to relieve the pain.

It is imperative to understand that you do not need to know how to draw or paint to make use and avail of this form of healing. It is probably better if you have never held a paintbrush at all. Most of my paintings were done using my hands only with no use of brushes.

The Benefit and Power of Heart Art 'Magic'

The feelings you experience as you apply the colour and the paint onto the paper allows the **Expression** to come to the surface, as this emerges; it takes on a life of its own. Trust the process and go with the flow. This expression can help you to understand the **Feeling** that you experience as you paint the picture. When you experience the feeling it can bring up memories instantly or it can take time for you to **know** and

understand what the memory 'linked to the feeling' is all about.

This expression or self-expression is linked to self-acceptance. Self-acceptance is huge. It can literally transform your life and bring great joy. When you learn to accept yourself, this is a starting point to work from. If you don't like what you **See/Feel/Know** about yourself you can make changes, start with small steps on your Life Ladder. Making small steps can lead to bigger achievements and start a positive cycle. When you live in this way, it can give you the freedom to live in the moment. Freedom in life is a wonderful way to live in your day. The freedom starts in your head first before it transforms into your heart and body and finaly effect your daily life.

Chapter 8 - How Heart Art Helped Me to Make Changes

Progress is impossible without change; and those who cannot change their minds cannot change anything. *George Bernard Shaw*

This is the beginning of the end, of my healing journey

I have had an amazing journey using the Heart Art 'Magic' painting process. It has literally been a saving grace at the most challenging times in my life. I still find it an incredible way of helping me make changes and it facilitates me in a very gentle and effective way. Heart Art 'Magic' has brought me to the stage that I can share my journey and experience with others, and help them to discover the 'inner direction' that is waiting to be told and exposed for a happier outcome and a lighter life attitude.

I am so grateful that I was given this opportunity to experience this way of working and will never forget my mentor Marie Perret who facilitated me during this period. Marie shared her own experience of her spontaneous painting, when she came to Ireland to run these workshops.

Heart Art 'Magic' helped with my pain and eventually my 'pain relief'. Marie is a wonderful inspiration. If she had kept this information to herself I would not have learnt all I did and it has enabled me to become much stronger physically, emotionally, mentally and spiritually. It has been instrumental and life changing for me. I eventually found the reason WHY I was attracting these negative experiences into my life. Heart Art 'Magic' set me free.

I have created over one hundred paintings in my Heart Art 'Magic' healing process, and I would like to share some of them with you. I would like to show you **how** this way of expression can 'heal the hurt' that we have learnt to bury within ourselves. We suppress these experiences that have upset us so much, and try to forget about them. But that never works. When we bury hurt inside, it festers, gets worse, and it needs to be extracted and released in some way. We can dwell on the problem or we can deal with it. When we address it we can heal ourselves. Suppression leads to depression. I am sure that I was depressed as a very young child, after losing Tony, when my mother was trying to find out why I had no energy.

Paintings Flow Explained

I am sharing this flow of painting with you so that you can see the progression of how each one was a step forward towards my healing. Starting on page 39; this was the first Heart Art 'Magic' painting that I did. I have included a message which you might find helpful on the opposite page and I have also described how each painting had an effect on my physical, emotional, and mental or sprirtual being on the day that it was painted. Each painting had a profound effect on me and as the paintings flowed one after the other, my healing was like the layers of an onion, layer after layer peeled away until the core of my being was finally healed, energised and empowered.

You too can use these images as a reflection. Choose a painting to look at. Notice 'how you feel' as you look and observe which painting you choose. It would be a great exercise for you to write down how you feel, before you choose a painting. Write how you feel as you view the painting, and how you feel when you are finished reflecting on the painting. You will be amazed at how the colours and the image can have an effect on your mood and emotions.

Better still, get the materials and start your own Heart Art 'Magic' journey and find the wonderment that is hiding deep down within you. Before you start; find a connection to your inner self, and centre yourself. Ask for direction and guidance that will be appropriate for you at this time and sit in silence and wait for a feeling or a knowing. When you start meditation or connection it may feel foreign to you, but like every new beginning it is a learning process. Trust what comes and go with your own flow of what feels right for you. Love yourself through your 'Magical' journey of discovery.

"The object, which is the back of every true work of art, is the *attainment of a state of being*, a state of high functioning, a more than ordinary moment of existence...We make our discoveries while in the state because then we are clear sighted. – *Robert Henri The Art Spirit, 1923*

Meditation and Centering

Read over a few times and close your eyes and remember what comes to you as you take five to ten minutes to;

Find a comfortable position, close your eyes, and sit upright with your back against the chair. Feel your feet in contact with the floor. Notice how relaxed your body feels as it is ready to make the connection to light and guidance.

Imagine a light shining about a foot above the centre of your head. Sense and see this light shining down upon you and covering your whole body from the top of your head to the tips of your toes.

Take a deep breath in as the light shines brighter and brighter with each breath you take. Feel your body relaxing even more as you exhale and your body wants to sink deeper and deeper into the chair, as your breathing becomes more natural.

Imagine a beautiful pink light emanating from the light above your head and this pink love light shines down over your body from the top of your head to the tips of your toes. Breathing in the pink love light as it descends over you.

A wonderful blue healing light now wraps itself down over the pink love light from the top of your head to the tips of your toes.

Purple transluscent light shines down over the blue healing light, incorporating the pink love light, as it descends from the top of your head to the tips of your toes.

See the white, pink, blue, purple and now gold, protecting and sealing the cleansing, loving, healing, spiritual light that you are now connected to and guided by and bringing forth the essence of who you are and what you need to see to be free. Now, create your way to success and empowerment.

*P=Portrait and *L=Landscape = turn book clockwise

My Message:
Daily Inspiration is given, when you take the time out to connect to stillness. This stillness comes when you connect to your 'higher self', 'higher consciousness', 'higher power' or whatever your belief system is. You can visualise a flame or light source, about twelve inches above your head. See this extremely white shearing light and allow this light to shine down over your body, and covering you like a soft warm blanket. Feel and sense this happening and when you are ready **'LISTEN'**, **'SEE'**, **'FEEL'** what message is being delivered to you. Notice how you feel as you become **'Inspired'** in the stillness.

My Experience:
This is my first day and my first experience of Heart Art 'Magic'. Not knowing what to expect, I started this painting effortlessly and it just grew. I got lost in the detail. When I look at the finished painting, I see it as myself in the middle of the painting, represented by the yellow head.
The right hand side is darker both inside and outside the head, and yet there is a core of lightness emanating from the right hand. There is also a tremendous slashing of energy going from right to left ending in a swirl of a golden orb, which is continuing to swirl, catching dark negative energy and transforming it to brilliant yellow light.
I feel so grateful to 'be'. To be given this 'direction', 'inspiration', to be here and now and re-discover something about myself. I ask for this process to help develop ME with grace, gratitude, honesty, integrity, prosperity and Uuniversal Energy.

Circle of Life -* P

My message:

As you look within this circle of life, notice how you feel. How does the colour affect you? Look from the outside of this circle and let your gaze go to the centre, and from the centre let your eyes wander around and around, back out to the outer circle. Do you feel that you are going around in circles? Repeating the same mistakes? Are you going nowhere? Or is your life a beautiful circle of life.

My Experience:

In my meditation, I could see this circle of light emanating and growing outwards and back inwards as it reverberated backwards and forwards and the colours kept changing with this motion. As I painted it with my hands, going around and around, I could feel the movement right in the centre of my being. When I changed the colours, I felt the shift in my energy levels with each colour change. I ask that this circle of life brings about a balance that I need right now in my life. This painting was done in fifteen minutes or so. It flowed effortlessly and yet it happened really quickly and it was energising me at the same time.

Hands of Light -*L-

My Message:

Look at the hands, emerging from the darkness and grasping up and out, while reaching towards the light. Know that you are being lifted from your darkness, out of the place where you have stayed too long. It is time to take the hands of light and lift yourself upwards to feel a freedom that you so deserve. You can lighten the load that you have been carrying for far too long. You are meant to be free to enjoy life. It is your right.

My Experience:

This painting felt as though I was emerging from the deep darkness of where I had been living and my hands were beginning to lift me towards the light where I could see and breath. I feel that the painting is showing me that I can make a change and there is hope of a positive outcome. I need to take stock of my current situation, which is my starting point. I feel then I can see where this journey can bring me. Blue is a healing colour and yellow represents the emotional aspect in the body. I am looking forward to a positive outcome. I really need it right now.

My Message:

Look into the rainbow Sunset. What do you see as you stare into the depths of each band of colour? The colour itself will seep into the deepest part of your mind to bring you peace and restfulness, which you can bring with you into your day. Immerse yourself in the Rainbow Sunset. Feel the energy that you need for you, right now.

My Experience:

I loved painting directly with my hands. It gives me a new freedom with paint. I can feel the difference between using a brush and using my hands. I seem to get into the painting instantly. This painting gave me a feeling of ease in my body. I got lost in it and didn't feel my pain as much, when I was focused on what I was 'connected' to, and 'seeing' what was emerging. I had all the colours on the painting when I was 'inspired' to mix and merge the red and blue together and the mountains instantly appeared. This painting went from just being a band of colours and my mixing the colours of red and blue a landscape appeared within minutes. This rainbow sunset brings me into an ease and lightness that I really love experiencing.

My Message:

What do you need to get away from in order to feel free? Once you know what it is you are halfway there to the freedom that you can experience, when you make the right choice. What choices will you make? Will that mean stepping out of your comfort zone? Sometimes, our comfort zones hold no comfort at all. It can hold us back and keep us imprisoned in a negative state. Stretch yourself to step out of your comfort zone and this can enable you to blossom grow for you to be the the best that you can be. Make the right choice for your freedom.

My Experience:

I started in the right hand corner using black and blue. I was physically feeling as if I had gone a few rounds in a ring with a boxer. My body was extremely challenged at this point in time. This was 10th December, day 3, and I was enjoying this new experience of exploring a new way of 'being in touch' with what was going on with my body. I then I painted the white light 'exploding' from the darkness. It was then I felt inspired to paint the butterfly shapes. I felt 'lighter' as a result and it was a very nice feeling. I am beginning to really enjoy this experience.

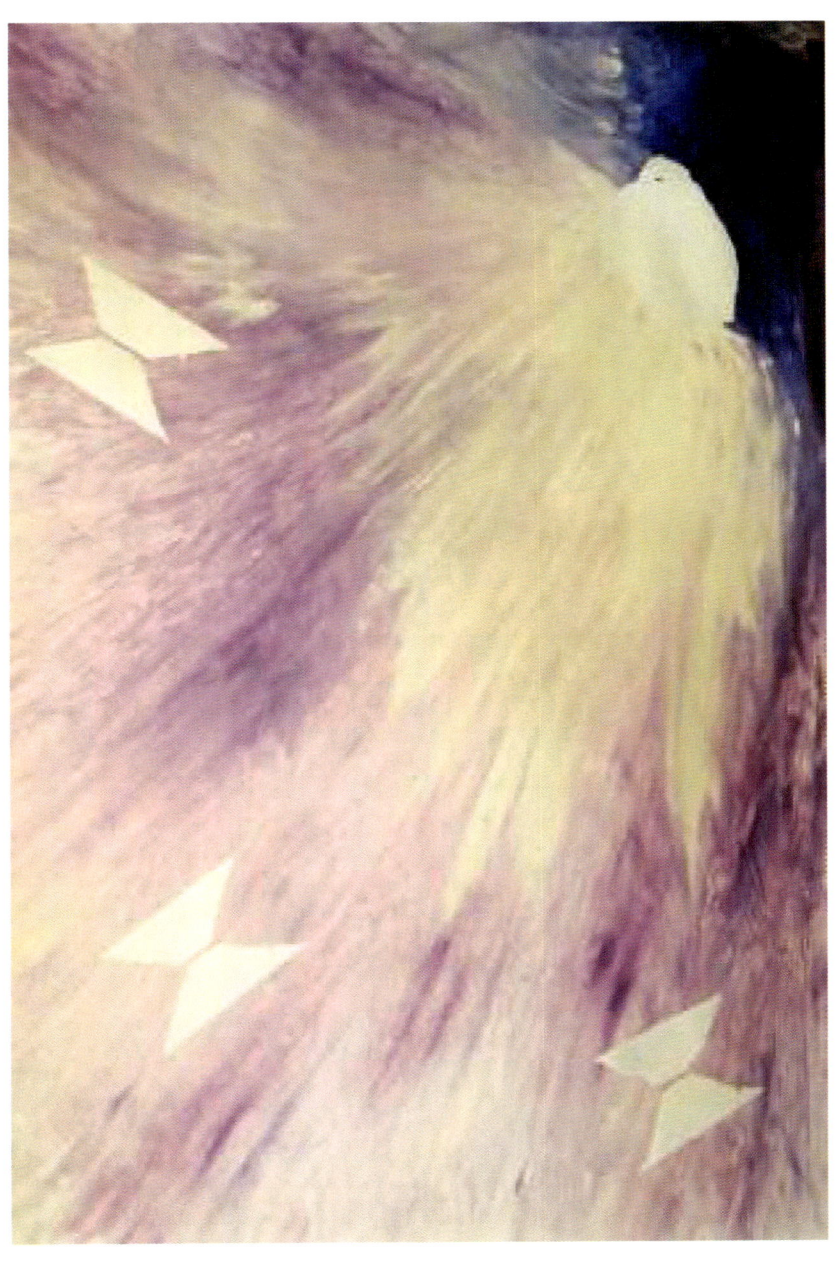

My Message:

When you claim your power and stay centered through every day living, it fuels your body and mind to increase your confidence and also boosts your self-esteem. But it is worth it at the end of the day. The more you live in your own power the easier it is to stay centered and focused. When you live this way you energise yourself. If you don't, you won't.

My Experience:

This was a pure pleasure and joy. I thoroughly enjoyed mixing the paint on the paper, colouring and exploring the message that was revealed to me. It looked like a group of people sitting and kneeling and conversing and having fun. It reminds me of an aboriginal group of people, speaking with a wisdom that is being passed on from one generation to another. Being at 'one' with the land and the sky and mother earth, in what nature can provide for us. We can do more than just 'function' every day, by living our lives to the full. We can explore life, have fun and 'live in the moment'. This choice is a pure freedom in itself.

My Message:

Anger fuels anger. When you are angry, you attract more anger. There is only one way to stop this negative cycle and that is to think about all the things in your life that you are grateful for. Number one is the fact that you wake up in the morning, no matter how bad you feel, this is a wonderful start to your day. Be grateful for the air that you breathe, the food that you eat. It does not matter how 'bad' your situation is. Start focusing on the positive aspects of every day. Stop focusing on what is wrong. This will stop your negative cycle and start reversing the process. Do it and notice the changes you can make.

My Experience:

This really represented what I was feeling at the time. I was in extreme pain and I felt great heaviness in my body. I lashed the paint on with my hands using a lot of red and yellow. Red represents the base chakra and where we hold a lot of anger issues. I was certainly feeling angry because I was not making progress with my physical body. While the painting was still wet I took a palette knife and made slashes upwards and outwards. This reminded me of a forest that I was trying to cut through personally. I didn't expect to find myself so physically challenged yet again. Early in 2003 I was fitter than ever. Giving fitness classes and running my clinical practice and having a freedom in my body. I am now dependent, yet again, on my family to help me get through my day.

In the Midst - *L

My Message:

Are you in the midst of change, or do you need to be? What area of your life could do with a positive change, and how could you go about making that change happen. This may be a good time to make a little tweak in the direction that could set you free. If you choose to make that decision, know that you are never on your own when you make a change that is for your good and the good of all of those around you. You will be glad you did, when you reap the rewards.

My Experience:

I worked a lot of colours in this painting. It was very insignificant to me and I felt quite detached from it. I am physically worn out and it is affecting my emotional and mental state as well at this point in time. When I stood back and looked at the painting I felt lost and it looked as though I was in the midst of something and not knowing what that represented. Even though I consciously do not understand this representation, I know that my subconscious has an exact understanding and a belief that I will get this message at a level that I can deal with in this present moment. I am just going to go with it, accept and trust that the outcome will be in my favour.

Painful Separation – In FULL Separation -*P

My Message:

Where would you paint your pain? What part of your body is affected? How does this make you feel? When you write it out or paint it out you can feel a difference starting to happen. Notice how it makes you feel before you do this exercise and how you feel after you do this exercise. You will be amazed at the difference. Is this your personal pain or are you carrying someone else's pain?

My Experience:

I am really struggling today. I feel as though I am about to lose control and scream. I decide to paint what my pain 'feels' like. In my meditation today I could see these skull shapes coming at me from a deep dark blackness. I remember these from a nightmare I had as a young child. They terrified me then, as I didn't understand what they were at the time. They are undermining me now, because I do know what they represent and I am scared for my future and what it holds. This painful challenge that I am experiencing is sometimes too much to bear. Today is one of those times. As I paint the pain, it is like a roaring fire within me, screaming and voicing 'I am here'. I decided to add a lighter side to my body as I painted it out and I added a great white movement on the right hand side, to represent the movement I will feel when my body is healed. I am taking control through the painting to show that "I KNOW what this outcome will be, because I claim a freedom for ME". I am in charge now, and so be it. I will have FULL separation from this pain; I know it and I claim it right NOW

My Message:
Come into your sanctuary where you can relax and rest, as you soak up the elements of the air, water, wood, metal and fire. All these elements know what to do in your body, and they do it naturally, just as nature intended. You consciously do not need to know what these elements can do for you. Just TRUST the process and enjoy the healing that you allow to take place when you see yourself sitting here. Your 'Sanctuary', your place of healing, your place to enjoy your timeout as you visualise your dreams coming true.

My Experience:
This was a pleasure and a joy to paint. I totally got lost in it and could see myself, sitting back and relaxing in a peaceful place of tranquility where I can go to anytime I wished to find Peace and Harmony. My body felt more at ease after this. It was as if by painting the pain previously, it was exposed and out on paper and no longer had the powerful pull it once had on me. This was coming to my conscious awareness, and as it did so, I could see how I could have more control over how I am feeling in the present and in the future. This is a great insight that I have just experienced. I can bring this powerful thought process with me and live it every day. I realise that my mind is so much more powerful than my body. My mind is the conductor of my body. When I give myself the time to 'Train My Brain' for the outcome I need, I will progress faster.

My Message:

Reflect on the colours and the movement of moving up and connecting to Spirit. In Spirit we become 'INSPIRED', where we can just 'BE'. We are 'human beings' not 'human doings'. With Iinspiration we can trust the outcome in our lives and it becomes a pleasure to 'Go with the Flow'. You can now go into your 'Inner Direction' mode. Feel, be and see yourself being 'uplifted' to where you want to be in life. When you feel 'uplifted', you no longer feel 'down'. Enjoy this powerful process as you excel and reach the goals that you want to achieve in your life.

My Experience:

I used both hands at the same time and painted up and outwards, using blue and yellow which mixed in as green. This felt great and a sense of flow and freedom transpired. I added red and felt the movement of upwards and outwards uplifting. When I stood back to look at the painting I could see a white light emanating up from the base and rising to the top. Then I saw the outline of a head and shoulders, which I outlined in the green. I felt in touch with my spiritual body and it was showing me that getting into a meditative state allows me connection to my spiritual side, which is attempting to give me the inner direction I need. But, when I am not connecting daily, I can miss the message that I need to hear, and therefore I can experience pain and discomfort. I felt a wonderful comfort and a floating feeling when I was finished this painting. I love this way of working.

Chain Reaction -*P

My Message:

Think of what has been happening in your life just recently. Can you see a chain reaction link in a series of events? Remember what you think about you bring about. When you are thinking good thoughts, good things happen to come your way. When you think negative thoughts, negative vibrations will follow you around and set off a chain reaction of negativity. Change your thoughts and you can change your outcome. It really is that simple. Do it and see and feel the change

My Experience:

I used a brush this time to paint this. I started off with a colour and made a shape, and then another and another. Using different colours each time for each shape, I found I started to interlink them and worked away until I stood back and instantly thought of a chain link. I named it chain reaction, as I felt it was a direct reflection of the previous five paintings combined. Anger, feeling lost in the midst, in full separation of pain bringing me to my sanctuary and being guided freely when I connect = chain reaction. I feel the need to stay connected in meditation and stillness.

Vibration of life - *L

My Message:

Is your life going at a rhythmic pace or is it stop, start, stop and start. Stuck? Slow, or no go? Life flows from the rhythm of the drums. See yourself being in tune to the rhythm and see and feel the new life that vibrates outwards and upwards towards you. Look at the movement from the drum coming up and out and moving over and back into the drum again. Feel this vibration of life in your body as you relax and allow this movement to flow within you. What new vibration do you need to create in your life right now? See it. Feel it. Give it energy. Give it life.

My Experience:

This painting really blew me away. I felt liberated at the end of this and it really had such a profound effect on me, it brought me to my knees. I ended up in tears of grief and also tears of joy. I felt a great relief at the effect it had on me. I had been listening to drum music during my meditation and that is what I painted with all the colours of the rainbow emanating from the drum. I felt an excitement as the colours flowed up, out and around. I wanted to show the 'vibration' I felt inside, so I painted over the colours with white. I stood back to look at the painting and was 'inspired' to put two little red dots (heartbeats) in the centre of the yellow spaces, one on the left and one on the right. It was at this point that I had an instant 'knowing'.
It seems crazy, but I knew **instantly**, that before I was born I had a twin, a twin who didn't survive and come into this world with me. See the two 'heartbeats' to the rhythm of the drum.

Head above Water- *L

My Message:
You can sink, swim or keep your head above water. What would you choose in your situation? What is happening in your life right now that you feel you are drowning in, or just surviving? Is keeping your head above water sufficient for you right now or would you like to be on dry land, where you can have that feeling of being and feeling extremely safe. What choices will you make today? What do you need to look at and where do you need to make changes? Are you ready to address your situation?

My Experience:

Using more red paint (anger) and lashing the paint onto the paper, wondering what this painting was going to reveal to me. I was in more pain now than I was since the last workshop. I had another surgery on my spine in March 2007. I wondered what the future would hold as I have been unable to work since my accident in October 2005. When I looked at this finished painting it looked as I was just about keeping my head above water. I feel I am existing everyday rather than living. I am extremely annoyed, angry and upset. I know I have the ability to feel better within myself. But there are times that I 'lose patience and lose control' and end up not being able to think straight. The pain is so consistent and never seems to ease or stop. I would love it if I could walk away from my body and feel free from the constant pain. The past few months have been a very challenging time. I thought that the recent surgery would have made a difference to my physical body. It has only made my situation worse. While painting my focus is on the paint and what I am doing. At the moment the painting is my one and only escape.

Camouflage - *P

My Message:

You can hide behind a mask and pretend to the outside world that ALL is okay in your world. Or you can claim a wonderful sense of freedom when you step out from behind your camouflage. Why do we sometimes feel the need to hide? What purpose does it serve? Are you hiding from yourself right now, or somebody else? There is no comfort in camouflage. It is easier and less painful to 'unmask' and have a good look at what you need to see. Clear out the wound you are living in and your body and mind can begin to heal.

My Experience:

I felt I was just going through the motions of this workshop. My heart wasn't in it and I wondered if I really should have come at all. The reason I did come this time was because the last workshop was so profound for me, and also the messages I got from it, and for what it showed me. This camouflage represented to me that I was 'hiding' from the 'real' me. I did not want to 'show' myself to the world, because I did not 'like' what I felt within. I felt I was a shadow of my former self. I used to be 'fit and active' and I used to love my work. I am no longer able to do any of those things and I feel extremely deflated and withdrawn from society. It is difficult to face everyday situations when I cannot operate physically. I know that I am putting a brave face on things at present in order to get through my day. But, I do not like it, it's false.

My Message:

When you look at this painting does it energise you? Absorb the colours of the wheels. Are they moving or are they stuck? Are you moving forward in life or are you stuck? What do you need to look at in your life to help you to move? Observe the cracks. Where are the cracks revealing themselves to you in your life? Write down quickly what thoughts come to you instantly. Don't think too long, just write quickly and spontaneously. This is a great way of making a change to motor you forward, if you need to move onwards.

My Experience:

This painting gave me a sense of "If I can't physically move, then I can do so through my paintings". These wheels of motion (again red =anger) are moving through a green (heart centre) band of colour with the fiery red and yellow at the top and bottom. The cracks that flow through the painting represent to me that I am growing, even though there are cracks showing at the moment, and that is okay for now. I am currently going through another 'University of Life Lesson' and that I will graduate with a great sense of 'wisdom' that will last an eternity. I am so grateful that I receive my wisdom with this way of working through this difficult time. It gives me a positive focus and helps to keep me going and achieving. It is a great way of moving forward at present.

The Big Bang - *L

My Message:

Life can be challenging. But sometimes when there is an explosion or upset, it can turn out to be a 'blessing in disguise' it can be the release that can set you free, when you allow it to. It may not feel like 'a wonderful event' at the time.
Every 'Big Bang' moment that I experienced in my lifetime turned out to be a powerful turning point that was so profound for me; it still amazes me to this day. I seem to have been able to turn negatives to positives with determination and drive. You too can always turn things around when you remain positive even in the throes of adversity.

My Experience:

Literally, the Big Bang occurred when I painted this. I felt as though there was a cosmic explosion within me as I progressed through this Journey of Heart Art 'Magic' while I am searching for answers. Something had definitely shifted within me as I painted this. I thoroughly got lost in the action of it and the outcome it could bring me, when I allow it to. I didn't know what the message was with this painting, other than I felt a great shift in my body as this painting progressed. Once again, my pain lessened, or I didn't notice it as much. When you 'sink' into the 'process' of the painting, it is an escape in itself. This is a great form of expression, with no planning and no expectations.

My Message:

Feel the strength start to emanate as you visualise yourself floating in this oasis of calm. The longer you stay in this peaceful place the stronger you become. The stronger you become the more your self-esteem grows and your confidence soars. Notice as you feel this strength energise your body and observe how it makes you feel. What kind of strength do you need now to make your life more rewarding?

My Experience:

This was heaven to paint. I could feel the serenity as I experienced this painting unfold. The calmness of the water, the strength of the tree, and the colour of the overall painting sapped right into the depths of my being and energised me inside. I felt a great sense of pleasure as I looked at the finished painting. It was wonderful to connect to these feelings, which over rode the pain I was experiencing at the time. This painting represents ease, peace and a strength that I know is deep down inside of me. I am stronger as a result of what is happening with my physical body. I am stronger in my mental and emotional body as my journey progresses. The painting points this out to me as I progress. I would dearly love my physical body to progress as well. In the meantime my paintings are fuelling me, energizing me and helping me every day. This in itself is what Heart Art 'Magic' represents to me.

My Message:

'Out of the dark and up into the light'. Lifting higher and higher towards the lighter side where things seem brighter each day. Each day brighter, each day lighter, when you choose how you want your day to be and how you wish to feel within yourself. Choice is so powerful when we use it. It is important to know what choices you need to make in your life to lighten and brighten it.

My Experience:

'Out of the dark and into the light' describes what I felt as I painted this. I felt I could 'fly free' from any situation when I can put my hands in paint and play with the colours and stand back and watch what can come forward. I enjoyed the flowers and the flow of the energy I felt as I had the feeling of being uplifted. I outlined the bird in Gold colour as I want to give this symbol a SOLID outline. I feel in time, I too can soar high and feel this outcome can happen for me. I look forward to it. I need it so much at this point in time. Yet I feel there is more that I need to see and feel before I can soar as HIGH as I want. I will have to wait and be patient before I know 'what it is' I need to know.

Emergence - *P

My Message:

Feeling ever more peaceful and stronger, you emerge to fill your day with positive choices and feelings. Emerging free and easy from situations you no longer want an association to. Feeling fully supported by those around you who are waiting in the wings. You can emerge triumphant in any situation when you know and claim the outcome you want. You need to be really specific and visualise your success.

My Experience:

The colours I chose represented how I was feeling on the last day of this workshop. Even though I was struggling physically and emotionally, the last few paintings had been inspiring for me. After applying the blue, yellow and green, I could see the head of a swan directly in the centre of the picture. As I brought this out, I began to see more and more little birds and butterflies emerging. I thoroughly enjoyed outlining these little beings fluttering and flying about. As this painting progressed, I felt the freedom of movement and flight. But, more importantly it showed me that I feel, at some point, I too can emerge from my present situation of pain and confinement. I am so looking forward to that day and hope it comes sooner rather than later.

Vision Circles - *P

My Message:

What is your vision for your future happiness? Are you happy within yourself or are you going around in circles. Know that you can 'make it or break it'. Create the vision within yourself that will bring about that vision. Let nothing prevent you from making it happen. Focus on your outcome and create a plan that allows you to achieve it. Only you can bring this about for you. Put your energy into it and keep going until it is yours.

My Experience:

I have had no improvement in my physical condition since the last workshop. I am very frustrated at my lack of progress. I start my painting instantly. Again the red comes out, but it is not as strong as before, it is more muted in tone and the movement is going around in circles. It is colourful and inspiring and it brings me joy. I feel inspired to paint infinity symbols all over the circles. This is a good start another new journey of my recovery. I know it will happen someday. I keep visualising myself being fit and mobile again. I really believe that I will someday be pain-free and be able to move easily. In the meantime, I will continue to paint and see what is coming to the surface, so that I can face it head on and allow my healing to be complete.

Seeds of Life - *L

My Message:

Sense the explosion of new beginnings as the seeds of life sprout and multiply. These Seeds of Life are flowing in all directions, upwards and outwards, over and over, again and again, in a never ending cycle. Creating inside of you the new beginnings of how you wish to feel every day. It is up to you, how you wish to energise that new life that you want to generate for you. Claim your future now as your seeds of life reach fertile ground and blossom and grow. Visualise it, see it, feel what it would be like to live your dream.

My Experience:

When I started painting with blue and yellow. I saw, what I thought was a big flower head. I started to outline the petals with red, but found as I progressed that it wasn't petals, but it looked more like seeds to me. The seeds started to flow out from the centre, and flowed outwards and downwards and dropping off, ready to sprout into new life. A new life is what I need to experience right now, and look forward to seeing what else will spring up for me in the next few paintings.

My Message:

How fulfilled do you feel right now? Is there a missing link in your life, which would help to energise you to be the best that you can be. What would that mean for you? What would you need to do to fill in that link to 'complete' and make you 'whole' and get you operating at your optimum potential.

My Experience:

After painting the background I took a palette knife and painted the red, green and brown. I just painted randomly, not feeling any connection. I was feeling pretty sorry for myself and not too enthusiastic about my day. It has been particularly stressful taking care of myself while I am here. I realise how much my family do for me when I am at home. When I stood back and looked at the finished painting I could see that I had omitted to link some of the colours together. What link am I missing? What do I need to 'look at' to connect to my 'inner self' so that I can 'fully' function as a person, a wife, and a mother? I really need to get my life back on track. I wonder what my missing link is; I hope that it will be revealed to me as I progress through this relaxing way of working with colour.

My Message:

Do not be afraid to face your fears. When you embrace them, you can see them for what they are. Sometimes they seem more fearful than what they truly are. You can be conditioned by your upbringing and you may have inherited fears that are not yours at all. When you face your fears you can liberate yourself and feel totally free.

My Experience:

I had started this painting and what was emerging was a bunch of flowers and it just did not seem right to me. I felt as though I was not painting what needed to come out. I could see a face appearing in the picture, and I just did not want to paint a face. So I continued with the flowers and was ignoring the face. I knew if I continued to ignore what wanted to show itself, then I was being untrue to myself. So, I stopped painting the flowers and concentrated on painting out the face. It was not a pretty face; in fact it looks quite scary and frightening. I am glad that I did, and I feel I am now being true to myself, as I need to 'face my fears' if I want to my body to heal totally. I wonder what is it I need to face. Will it present itself at this workshop? How long will I have to wait before I know what my fear is and what wants to present itself?

My Message:

This is your paradise retreat, a place of peace and inner tranquility. Listen to the birds singing and the water is making rippling sounds as it flows. This is a calming place to be today. Take these qualities and let them reside deep down inside you, enabling a serenity to seep into the core of your being. Revitalising and rejuvenating you fully, to be the best that you can be and feel.

My Experience:

After every storm there is calm period. After 'facing my fear' my calmness was restored by my paradise retreat. The colours helped enormously, the trees instilled strength within me and the water was calming and serene. The bird gave me a great message as it showed me to be big and strong, and not to fear anything that comes my way. It is portraying a confidence by showing its back to the world. It is showing me that I can be 'bigger' than I am today. And that I can fly away when I want to, or stay and revive myself any time I feel the need. The choice is up to me 'how I feel' and 'how I want to be'. My life can be a paradise, when I think of it as paradise. What I think about, I bring about.

Transformation - *P

My Message:

Transform, transform from cocoon to butterfly. From being earthbound to flying free from any boundaries that may be holding you back. The strength of this vortex lifts you up and the subtle flight of the butterflies helps to transform you into a Powerful and Peaceful Being. You can transform when and if you want to.

My Experience:

I loved this. It was effortless and enjoyable. The background came extremely fast and I could see this vortex rising up with a tremendous white light bursting out of it. It felt as though it could have a strength I could claim and use. Then, I saw a butterfly soar up and out of this vortex. It represented a butterfly transforming from an earthbound cocoon into a beautiful light creature of flight, that is free to go anywhere with ease. I claimed this transformation as my own. I feel a transformation deep, deep down inside of me starting at cellular level. I now need to wait until it grows strong enough to go from cellular level to fuel my physical body to function at my optimum and fullest potential. This painting is the final one of this workshop. It is a nice way to end and a great message to bring home with me.

My Message:

You can hold this torchlight in your body and mind to show you the way that is easier and straightforward. It can also lighten your day. The strength of this Olympic torch can have a tremendous impact on how you can see your way to how you can feel, in your physical, emotional and mental body. Hold the image in your mind and see it lighting your way to freedom.

My Experience:

The beginning of another four days and I am not sure how I am feeling physically. The restriction in my body is still the same and it is not getting any easier. It is still difficult to walk and stand and I really don't know how much longer I can keep my head above water. Heart Art 'Magic' is helping me stay sane and giving me comfort.

My first painting is a nice revelation, Olympic Torch, lighting my way. I know, and BELIEVE that I can get through this challenge. Heart Art 'Magic' is providing me with an outlet to relieve the tension in my mind and body. I will keep this Olympic Torch lighting my way as I discover what I need to know, so that I can set myself free for my wellbeing.

Nurturer of Nature – Giving Strength, Grace and Agility - *P

My Message:

See the gentleness behind the strength of Jigsaw and Cheeky Charley. If you could have their strength, grace and agility in your mind and body, to move forward easily, what would you see yourself doing? Don't hold back. It is time to claim your own strength and be the best the best that you can be.

My Experience:

This was a wow factor for me. When I started painting it, I could see a horse's head looming out of the picture and instantly I decided that there was no way I could paint a horse or that I would want to. So, I took the paintbrush and used the wooden end of it to scratch out a pattern on the already wet background. As far as I was concerned it was finished.
When I sat back and looked at it again, the horses head had appeared again, but this time it was facing the other direction. The eyes, ears and mane were all there. I outlined them and painted the mouth. I named her Jigsaw. Then I saw the foal, tucked underneath and I outlined and christened him Cheeky Charley.
I clearly understood that these paintings are not about what 'I want them to be'; they are about what is 'being shown to me'. And I am not to ignore what I see, when I see it. Heart Art 'Magic' is about the Process I experience; it is not about the finished Product. This was a wonderful lesson and I am open to I learn more.

Yipee De Do Da!!! – Celebration of Life's Freedom - *L

My Message:

Life is a celebration, even when you are not functioning at your optimum. When you live your life in gratitude, you can make significant changes to your current situation. The Law of Attraction is quite powerful. What you think is what you attract in your life. It is important to think about what you want to bring about. When you have good thoughts you attract good things into your life. Equally, when you think negative thoughts, you will attract negativity. Remain positive always.

My Experience:

There was no rhyme or reason to this painting. I just enjoyed the process and concentrated on the detail and outlining it. Because I was so focused I could lose myself in it and was not giving my physical condition the attention that it was demanding at this time. This is not easy, but it can help enormously. Today it helped, and I am so grateful for any little help. I literally played with the paint and the brushes and had a bit of fun. It was great, Hence the title of the painting, Celebration of Life's Freedom. I don't need an event to celebrate. Everyday can be a celebration in its own right.

Depths of Being - Where I can feed myself spiritually - *L

My Message:

Are you feeding yourself spiritually? Do you do it every day? Connecting deep down within yourself to hear the direction that you are being given, but then you don't take the time to LISTEN. Are you hiding in these depths and staying there because it is easier to be there than show yourself to be who you truly are?

My Experience

Again the dark colours emerged as it represented where I was at today. It is the second last day of this workshop. After applying the black and blue, (significant of how I was feeling) I saw a shape emerge and painted it out. Then I saw another, and another and this process just kept on going.
I spent a few hours over this painting, looking to see what else wanted to show itself. I was truly immersed in it and I felt I went into a great depth deep down inside myself. There seemed to be sea anemones' as well lurking in these depths so I painted them in. When I was finished, my body felt so much lighter. It is strange to think that painting in this way can have this effect, but I am so grateful for this lightness.

In the Distance – Enjoy being still in the present (Now = Won) - *P

My Message:

I have realised that stillness is a key to the most powerful connection, which brings peace and joy. It is similar to 'plugging in' to energise your body 'fully', so that you can be 'in charge' of how you feel on any given day. Even though you may be experiencing 'pain' in your body, this is a positive way of changing that 'circuit'. When you live in the now, you have won.

My Experience:

All my paintings are a blessing, and this one had another profound message to show me. It was surreal and I received a great relief as I painted this. As I looked into the distance in this, I felt a great balance and strength between the trees in the foreground and a sense of 'living in the moment'. When we live in the moment, that moment is NOW. When you reverse the letters NOW = WON. When we live in the moment, we have WON. When we learn to BE we can progress faster in life than if we KEEP DOING all the time. We are human BEINGS not human DOINGS. A brilliant lesson for me to keep living in the moment, when I do, I have won.

Trilogy – At one with Heart and Mind = Unity of Self - *P

My Message:

Stay in connection to your 'Inner Self' in order to be whole, physically, emotionally, mentally and spiritually. When you do, you will function better and feel better. Be true to yourself. Walk your talk and believe in what you do. Beliefs are like scaffolding; build them up to support you. The more you believe the more you achieve. Your beliefs are transformed as you grow and live your truth. They strengthen every day and support you in every way.

My Experience:

The last painting of this workshop appeared quickly. I used grey and watered it down significantly and brushed it on with a big brush. The Face on the left was the first one I could see. It was perfectly formed with neck and shoulders. Then I saw the face at the top of the painting and finally the face on the right. The hearts were already there and just needed the colour to bring them out.
What it showed me was, I needed to stay 'connected to my inner self' in order to be whole, physically, emotionally, mentally and spiritually. When I do, I will function better and feel better. I will be true to myself. I Walk my talk, believe in what I do. Beliefs are like scaffolding and our beliefs are transformed as we grow and live our truth. Creativity helps me to understand the value of life.

My Message:

Always go with your gut feeling. It is your inner 'intuition'. Your internal 'gut' is telling you what 'is' right for you, or what it is 'not' right for you. You can TRUST your GUT. It will not let you down. Go with this feeling always and you will be following your intuition. Your outcome will be the right one for you.

My Experience:

I am so physically worn out at this stage; I do not know how much longer I can put a brave face on things as I go through daily life. I have decided to have more surgery which will happen next month. When I painted this, I felt physically sick and emotionally worn out from the constant draining pain in my body. A physical churning in my gut, not knowing what the outcome would be, but it will be what it is meant to be. Expressing the feeling is an outlet for self-acceptance. Expression is linked to self-acceptance. Self-acceptance is huge. It is a starting point. Always go with your gut feeling.

My Message:

We all experience pain in life, whether it is a physical, emotional, or mental pain. There are also painful relationships to consider, with partners or parents, siblings or business partners. What type of pain are you experiencing at present? What do you need to do to change it?

My Experience:

This is what my pain looked like. It was like this spike being driven into the core of my being and it was disabling me from my physical ability and draining my mental capacity. It takes a lot of energy to 'hold' pain in the body. Not that I want to (hold the pain) but that is what is happening right now and I need to deal with it, while I can still control it. I had to sit down a few times while I painted this. My pain was intense during the process and I felt the urge to paint what the pain would look like. When I finished this painting the intensity of the physical pain had decreased. I am finding it amazing that using paint, plus getting in touch with the feeling in my body and expressing what wants to come up and out, and reveal itself on the paper, can have such a positive effect on my physical, emotional and mental state.

My Message:

When you see this painting, feel the peace and calmness wash over you, even as these little tornadoes flip and flap about. They can stir up emotions that you need to look at, so that you can have a wonderful balance within you. Always remember the owl is there to give you wisdom, advice and balance every day.

My Experience:

Black and blue again, bringing me into another depth of feeling. I could see these explosions happening after I painted the main one in the centre of the picture. There were more little beings and animals showing themselves as I painted them in. Just as I was coming to the end I saw this little owl, just hanging on the end of the biggest vortex. The owl represented a wisdom that I need at this moment. And he was perfectly balanced in the middle of the picture.

When the painting was finished, I felt really ill, it was six in the evening and I could feel my energy dropping fairly instantly as soon as I had finished for the day. I went straight to bed. I was so unwell, I could not even get ready for bed, I fell into it, and I didn't get up till the following morning. I had a disturbed night up until 1pm when I then fell asleep. The night seemed very short, once I slept. I woke the next morning feeling drained and lifeless, but at the same time calm and centered. At this stage I really needed to get some food for energy, as my last meal was lunchtime the day before.

Reflection - *P

My Message:

Remember to take some time every day to reflect on what you want to bring into your life. It instills calmness and serenity and strengthens your inner direction to get the best outcome for you. When you connect, you can detect what is happening within yourself. You then have the choice to change what you would like. Be the change you want to see in your life and enjoy the process.

My Experience:

This painting showed me I had to sit and reflect on all that I am experiencing. Meditating is going to help me to heal. I felt an inner calmness after the previous night and this painting allowed me to get into a flow of what was to come. It was light and easy and didn't take long to finish. I felt better after it. . I realise how important it is for me to 'create the space' to STOP, LOOK and LISTEN, to my MIND and BODY of what the possibilities are for me in life, WHEN I take the time to 'TUNE IN' to W11FM (what's is in it for me) Taking, receiving and accepting the 'guidance' I am looking for. Then, go with the guidance and enjoy doing what is right for me.

My Message:

When you know, you can grow. Awareness is the key to freedom. When you are in control, you can control your actions and therefore your outcome. When you think good things, good things happen. When you focus on the negatives, negatives happen. It is important to change a negative thought, then and only then, can you change the pattern and turn it around.

My Experience:

As I painted this I felt a sense of growing internally, which got me in touch with the core of my being. This showed me that I was in control, and when I can control my thoughts, I can control my actions and outcomes. When you think good things, good things happen. When you change the thought, you can change the pattern, when you change the pattern, you can change the outcome. I feel something good is going to show soon. I felt more at ease when I finished this painting.

Watching Movements - *P

My Message:

Keep watching within yourself to make sure that you know what is happening. An eyeful watch will keep you motivated in your journey through life and then you can be the best that you can be. This can create a wonderful internal environment within you for contentment. Notice what is 'looking' to present itself to you

My Experience:

This gave me a sense of being within my own cathedral and I am being watched from within. I could see this eye looking out at me and when I painted it, I could see another eye and another and then more eyes started appearing all over the painting. I felt I needed to keep watching within myself (meditation) to reveal my outcome. To notice what is 'looking' to come out. I look at 'watching movements' whenever I want to meditate. I can slip into a deep state and connect very easily and freely. I felt uplifted after this painting.

Keeping Tranquility - *L

My Message:

Serenity and tranquility fills you as you go deep within this painting. Feeling uplifted with the calmness of the water and the strength of the trees. Feeling uplifted is linked to Intuition / Inspiration, meaning being 'in touch' with Spirit. When you connect your expression to your feelings you are opening up to your Inner Direction. This will reveal your direction. When you follow this direction, you cannot go wrong. It will be correct for you, and you feel that it sits comfortably and goes flowingly. There is nothing like this wonderful connection, it feels great.

My Experience:

I felt really calm and relaxed as I painted this. My body was so much at ease after the turmoil I had felt at the beginning of this workshop. I felt I had transformed from Turmoil to Peace. This peace seemed to seep right into the centre of my being. I had the feeling of having released a blocked energy that gave me a new freedom in myself. When I felt so sick after painting 'Wisdom in Balance', it had obviously released something deep down within me that was holding me back. It was worth feeling so ill so that I could allow my body to release this blockage. I could feel and enjoy the freedom in my whole being, body / mind / spirit. Tranquility reigns deep down inside me and sets me free. I loved the feeling I got as I painted this and I love and appreciate the feeling I have now that it is finished.

My Message:
I challenge you to feel a great sense of 'going with the flow' and 'being in the moment' as you immerse yourself in the colours of this painting. Look at the small detail and get a sense of being sure that you know that, when we look closely at what we need to see, we make better choices in life. You need to stop sometimes to evaluate where you are in life, where you would like to be, and how you are going to get there. Start by looking at the big picture of where you would like to be. Then you can look at the smaller details of how you are going to achieve your dream. Sometimes you are unclear as to what you really want to achieve in life, and you drift along like a sailboat without a rudder or a sail. You need to hoist your own sail and decide what your direction is and what you want your life to be.

My Experience:
The final painting of this workshop just flowed. I used vibrant beautiful colours with a movement that allows me, to feel that feeling within my body. I felt a great sense of 'going with the flow' and 'being in the moment'. I got lost in the detail of the painting as I took a small brush and painted small details up and around the picture. The details are important in life, as it is in the detail of everyday living that creates the bigger picture in life.

It was a great way to finish off the workshop. It never ceases to amaze me at how many different paintings present themselves each time. And the meanings they show me are so profound. I felt so much better at the end of this workshop. Another healing has happened, another layer shifted and I feel so much lighter in myself.

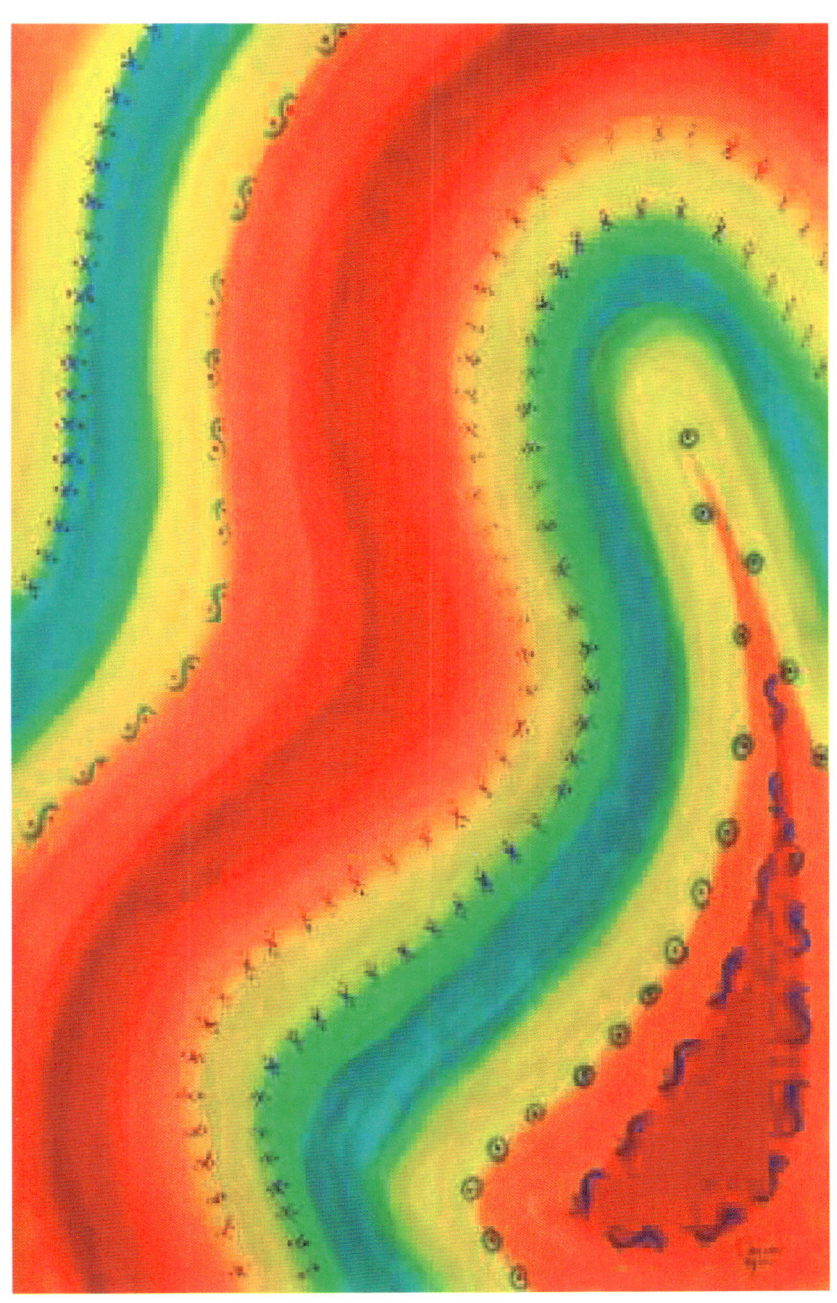

Creative Explosion - *P

My Message:

What do you see as you look at this creative explosion? Notice how your body feels as you get in touch with the colour and the movement of what you see. What do you want to create within yourself? What new life do you want to experience as you begin to get in touch deep down within you and know what you want to achieve.

My Experience:

This painting was a great experience. I am still in the early stages of recovery from another spinal surgery which I had last month. The dreadful restriction I had experienced over the past year is now released. The pain is still present and the new pain from surgery is lingering. I had an implant put in my back to help me walk with ease. I dreaded the fact that I needed more surgery, but I could not go on the way I was and eventually took my doctor's advice. Walking was too painful no matter how gently I attempted to take easier strides.

When I stood and looked at the colours I had painted in these little seedlings of movement, it represented 'new life' being released all over and going everywhere. It was great to be back painting again with this new sense of release in my body. I wonder what I will be shown this time around. It is great to be here to experience more expression of what needs to show up in my paintings.

My Message:

To engage in change, you need to know what change you need to make. Where are you at in your life right now? Are you living your dream? Are you happy, content? Or, are you unwell and frustrated with yourself and your situation? When you know you're starting point, and then you can know what you need to change, you begin to flow as you grow.

My Experience:

I really enjoyed this one, it just flowed so easily and I totally got lost in the experience and the colours. I had seen these colours in my meditation before my painting. I knew what I was going to paint before I finished going deep down and connecting internally. I could see the spirals whirling and twirling in all the different colours. I was experiencing the movement in my body as I painted each circle. It was a wonderful feeling and I also felt a great excitement bubbling up inside of me as I went through the motions. I felt much better physically than I had earlier. Each time I looked at this painting, I could recall and FEEL the ease that I had experienced while painting this one. It has had a profound effect on me, and still does today. I use it regularly for my meditations.

'Five Elements' Strength in Stillness -*P

My Message:

Look into the stillness and feel that stillness in your body and mind. Feel the heat of the sun soaking in through the pores of your skin. The mountain grounds and steadies you fully. When you look at the tree, notice how you too can feel your roots emanating from the soles of your feet and going deep into the centre of the earth. The water is a cleanser, which can help you wash away all negativity from your body, leaving you steady, grounded, lighter and positive in every aspect of your life.

My Experience:

After the last painting I felt really light and in a good mood. In this painting I used turquoise and white to paint the background. I had two paintbrushes going at the same time. There was a nice flow to it as it progressed and unfolded. When I stood back to look at it I could see a rocky mountain on the left hand side. Then I felt inspired to paint the tree on the right hand side. Earth, Fire, Water, Air and Metal. I used a lot of gold paint to highlight the areas that stood out for me. All of the five elements combined into this painting. To me it spells strength and also has a beautiful strength in the stillness.

Protected invitation to the Light - *P

My Message:
As you imagine yourself walking through this forest towards the beautiful strength of the sunlight, you notice how more relaxed and energised you feel. The further you 'see' yourself going into the woods, the deeper the relaxation you experience. The deeper you allow yourself go the more energised you will feel. Know that you are fully protected as you go deeper and deeper. The deeper you go the more protection your body draws into itself.

My Experience:
Today, one month, ago my mother in law passed away. Last night as I lay in bed reading I heard someone approach my bed. My back was to the door as I heard footsteps coming closer to me. A hand reached out to me and tugged the sheet, three times in succession. I froze, and found that I could not move. I hadn't heard the door open I could feel a presence in my room. After the tugging on the sheet I felt a hand resting on my back. I couldn't do anything; I think I was also holding my breath. I had to wait until I built up the courage to look and see who it was. I turned around slowly to find the room empty. It was a really weird experience. I felt that this was my mother in law letting me know that all would be okay, for her and also for me. I felt she was ready to now go into the light and be free.

This painting is for her; as I see her being fully protected as she wanders off to the light. She died on the anniversary of her son, who passed away 21 years ago to the day. After I finished painting it, I was standing quietly with my eyes closed and I could feel a hand resting on my shoulders. Similar to what I had experienced the night before, except this was a light touch, with no tugging. It felt as if she placed her hand there to say "I am off now, everything is okay".

My Message:

You can view this vortex as a positive or negative energy. What is within you that is bursting to come to the surface? Write down what instantly comes into your mind. You can use the power of the vortex to revitalise you or you can see it as draining your energy. Decide what you would like it to be for you. Do you wish to be energised by them or stay in a negative frame of mind and allow your energy to drain away?

My Experience:

This is the start of another new workshop and a beginning of a new change for me, although I didn't know it at the time. I could not begin to imagine what was to come. My first painting came very fast, one vortex after another presented quite quickly. As my hands went around and around, I could feel the lightness in my body as I painted each vortex. I felt lighter and lighter and the swirls of colour flowed really, really easily. It still amazes me that all this creativity is deep down within me and bursting to come up to the surface. The more I do this work the deeper I go into my subconscious where new revelations are there to be explored and understood. I am excited about what will come to the surface this time.

My Message:
What do you feel as you look into this picture? Are you in the 'dark', coming into the light? What part of your life needs to be lightened up? How do you think you would 'feel' when things are lighter, in your body/mind? Why do you think you are in this situation? Is this your problem or does it belong to someone else? What do you need to do or change in order to make these corrections?

My Experience:
When I started this painting I could feel the urge to paint a tree. I had started on the left hand side of the paper and the tree started to appear. Trees seem to appear quite often in my paintings. I love them and thought that this was my urge to paint a tree. I stopped myself from painting and had a word with my mentor Marie. I explained what I was feeling to her and she suggested I take different colour paint and start again and see what progressed. I started again using black and blue and worked my way up the left hand side. I put on the black and blue with my hands and once again the tree came out, there was no way I could stop it. I realized at this point, that this is not what I want to paint; it's what wants to show itself to me. It is what Heart Art 'Magic' is all about. I am painting from my subconscious; it is not a conscious decision, so therefore I have no conscious control over the outcome. It is what it is, and that is what makes this way of working so exciting. I do not have to think about it. I just need to make and take the time to be still, connect to my inner self for a few minutes and then take the colours and paint what wants to come out, effortlessly.

Let's Party - *P

My Message:

Know that you can celebrate the most wonderful things in life. Celebrate being able to get out of bed in the morning, and all that you are able to do for yourself. Being able to dress and wash. Enjoy the weather, whether it is cold, hot, raining, snowing, windy or dry. Celebrate the simplest things that you may take for granted. When you are functioning at any level, life is a great party. It may not feel like it at the time, but remember, what you think about, you bring about.

My Experience:

Let's Party, made me realise that I have not been socialising or partying for the past number of years, since my accident. I have not had the inclination, energy or physical ability to enjoy going out. I liked the colours in this and the simplicity of the painting. It was a pleasure to do and it came really fast after the meditation this morning. It never ceases to amaze me how these paintings reflect what I need to see. They are a true reflection of what is missing in my life.

"Out of" or "Into" – I choose - *P

My Message:

What do see when you look deep down into the centre of the circle? Can you see the face looking out from the very centre? Notice, how do you feel as this presents itself to you? Do you feel you are going into the circle or coming out of the circle? Remember, you get to choose your outcome. When you choose your outcome, you are taking control of your life. When you are leaving it to chance, life is controlling you.

My Experience:

This is the second painting of this workshop. When I reflect on the message I got from the last painting, Let's Party, I realise that I need to be in control of the choices I make in life. If it's got to be it's up to me.
When I looked at this painting; Out of or Into, I didn't know if my vision wanted to go right down into the painting or whether my eye was drawn to come from the centre and look outwards. When I looked into the heart of it I could see the outline of a face with eye sockets and no eyes. I made the decision that I was going to decide what it was going to be for me. When life throws me a situation, I am going to decide how to take it. I can either see it as a positive or a negative, but it will be my decision. I am either coming out of something or going right down into it..

"Busy Busy Busy" – Take time out - *P

My Message:

This message is really important. Do not wait until it is too late before you take some vital time out for yourself. If you are too busy in life, stop for a few minutes to take stock of where you are right now. You may need to re-evaluate your position and what you would like to do to make changes. You either make the changes or the Universe will arrange some 'timeout' for you so that you are forced to stop involuntarily. When your body is not at ease, it is dis-eased.

My Experience:

When I started this painting I didn't want to use my hands or to use brushes. I used some sponged rollers and started with green and rolled the paint on with plenty of water. I then used yellow and finally red. I noticed how my body felt as this painting emerged and it felt really muzzy and confused. I was wondering what this was attempting to show me as I had started this workshop with Let's Party which I felt was a fairly positive message. I know from previous experience that when I do not take time for myself, it will be given to me.

There is no way that I need this right now. I need to take some time for me, to see what I need to look at. I need to do it sooner rather than later. I neither want nor would choose another' timeout', I have had enough.

My Message:

It is so important to have a balanced lifestyle with fun factored in. Fun can be whatever you want it to be. It does not need to be anything extravagant. It can be a walk in the woods. Maybe spending a day at the beach, visiting friends or just having a laugh. Do something that will be up-lifting. When you are in an uplifted mood, you will have a shift in energy towards a positive outcome.

My Experience:

I was really intrigued with this painting. It came so fast. I used my hands only and as I put on the white and blue background and worked it back and forth I could see the dolphin in the centre appear first. I used the blue paint only. It was amazing to see this life-form just jump into the painting so effortlessly. Then I stood back to look again and saw the dolphin at the top and finally the one at the bottom emerged. When I looked at the bottom one I could see a fourth dolphin in the shadows. It took only fifteen minutes for this whole painting to emerge. It came so fast and the message I received from it was to take time for fun. My life needs a balance of fun and excitement. It is not easy to factor this in when my pain levels are so high and my ability to move is not great. But, even doing this type of painting allows me to lose myself in the process so that I am not so focused on the pain. Pain versus Painting, I choose painting, which will win each time. It is so rewarding and fulfilling and energising.

"Secret Hideaway" – Escape When I Need To -*P

My Message:

Do you ever have the urge to hideaway to get away from it all? To find a sanctuary to escape to, so you can unwind. Our body and mind is our sanctuary and it is there for you to tap into instantly. All you need is peace and quiet. Sit or lie down, be still and go inside of yourself to find your peaceful place. A place so you can nurture, heal and feel free.

My Experience:

This picture is my great escape and a great hideaway to seek out and refresh myself when I feel like it. I started this painting with my hands and the lightness remained in the centre as the painting progressed. After I finished the centre I felt as though I needed to bring out some very dark colours in the foreground. Eventually, I could see the picture develop into lightness in the back and heavy foliage in the front. I switched to brushes and let the picture unfold. I can imagine myself here in this hideaway, as I allow my body to take what it needs to become the change I need to function.

Cellular Activity – Creating what I want at primary level - *P

My Message:

When you look at these circles, what do you see? What would you like these to represent for you. If you could create a new life for yourself, what would you design? What would you do that you are currently not doing now? You can be the designer of your new destiny. Have you decided what you want to bring into your life, or are you happy to drift along and see what you get. Sometimes we take more time to plan a holiday than we take to plan our life and what we want. It is important to be the Master of your Destiny. If you are not the Master, who is?

My Experience:

I enjoyed this one. I loved the colour and enjoyed creating the circles, and mixing the paint with my hands. It reminded me of new cell growth that I can create whenever I want to. I can change my way of thinking and being. I need to make changes, as I no longer want to feel the way I do anymore. I am tired of the restrictions that I am experiencing in my body. I need a new lease of life. It is up to me to decide what I want and how I wish to feel. I no longer leave it up to chance. I am taking the lead and going forward with what I want to create in my lifetime.

Let's Play - *P

My message:

What type of relaxation do you like? It can be travel or sports. Reading or writing. Painting and drawing. Or simply take some paper and doodle, making and drawing shapes. Making some fun with family and friends, playing games, or just socialise. Creating craft work, or just do something for you, that you like doing, and do it every day if you can. It will lighten your spirit and energise you. Take time to play every day.

My Experience:

In my meditation I could see these bands of colour and I felt a great sense of connection. I knew I needed to paint the bands of colour and as I did I had a great connection to a childhood memory. I could see myself about seven years of age sitting down drawing and colouring in the drawing. It was a picture of me running with a tremendous speed and I had captured the 'speeding motion' in the drawing. Because of my inability to walk with ease and no way of running (will I ever be able to run again?). I started painting the balloons and then the pram and the rest just happened as I progressed through onwards. The train and plane reminded me of travelling to different destinations. It gave me a sense of fun and play. I need to create some play every day.

My Message:

You can follow your dream, when you know what that dream is. What do you sense when you look into this scene? See yourself walking into this painted scene and create your dream from this serene backdrop. The deeper you go into this picture the more you know what your dream is. See it, feel it and claim it for you right now. You deserve it.

My Experience:

The feeling of rubbing the paint on the paper with my hand still excites me every time I do it. I never know what is going to 'present' itself to me. These paintings really are a PRESENT to me, not just having the paintings at the end, but the MESSAGE that I receive from the paintings.
The colours are so relaxing and calming. When I painted the trees, I could see the background merging away into the distance. I am having a great time with this painting workshop. I just love the messages that are pouring out through the paintings. Even though my body is experiencing pain and discomfort, I have been 'getting lost' in the process of my journey. This experience is showing me how valuable this 'Heart Art Magic' form is proving to be a blessing. I am so grateful that I can 'get lost' and enjoy myself.

Peaceful Place - *L

My Message:

Feel the silence within this snow scene penetrate right through to the core of your being. Total silence can be yours in this cool blue haven of cleanliness and calmness. Look into the pristine white snow mountains in the background, with cool blue water in the foreground. Shower yourself with positive energy in this Peaceful Place. Enjoy immersing yourself here and feel the essence of healing transport you to new heights

My Experience:

The urgency that I felt to do another painting before I go home today is huge. After dipping my hands in the colour turquoise and white together, the painting starts to emerge as always, but never the same outcome. This painting is calming me immensely. I did feel that I shouldn't have come on this workshop, because it meant I was missing celebrating my 35th Wedding Anniversary. Damien so understands and wanted me to come this time and continue my healing process. I truly am blessed and appreciate my family and friends who support me. I am so glad that I took the time to come and paint. It is giving me a wonderful release and 'painting a picture' of what is happening in my life right now, is so rewarding.

My Message:

Flowers bloom naturally and easily when the soil is good and full of nutrients. When the soil is devoid of nutrients, flowers will not thrive. What type of soil are you living in? Are you living on nutritious 'live' raw food or 'cooked' dead food? You are what you eat. Are you thinking positively and living in an energised way. What you eat and how you think and act, will determine the growth that you experience in life. Maybe it is time to reflect and see if you need to make a change for the better. What changes would you choose to empower yourself today.

My Experience:

I used a sponge roller with orange and two types of red paint and I covered the entire page. After which I saw a flower head which I outlined in yellow and the painting grew from there. I covered all the petals in gold. Gold is a sign of protection and wealth. Before I started this painting, I was feeling sick, in pain and quite miserable. By the time I had finished painting and doing all the flower heads, I was feeling lighter. The sick feeling had eased and I was totally pain free. It was wonderful. I do not know when was the last time I was free and easy in my body and mind. Being pain free is so wonderful. It is hard to believe that finally my body is at ease. I pray it stays this way.

My Message:

It is so wonderful to be in the stillness. This is where you can receive and believe that you are in control and no outside influence can steal your power from you. You have an incredible force-field of energy within you and around you that you have not been using to its optimum potential. It is time to use the stillness to receive the messages you are given daily, when you take the time to listen and learn.

My Experience:

The stillness is the key to setting me free. I so enjoyed this painting of expression. As I began to express what I was feeling the blue and green seemed to take on a life of their own and produced this painting effortlessly. It was so calming and relaxing. It flowed quite easily and I had a great sense of 'being in the moment' from beginning to end. Silence and stillness is huge, and in this day and age there are very few places you can be, that provides total silence. I feel my body grows stronger the deeper I go into stillness. I need to create the time in my day so that I facilitate myself into this new way of living.

Creative Explosions - *P

My Message:

What part of your life needs an injection of energy? If you could create something new for you what would it be? How would you go about creating it? See yourself as if you already have it. What you think about you bring about.

My Experience:

During my meditation this morning, I could see these explosions of colour bursting out like the Fourth of July celebrations. The colours were pastel and so bright, that they lit up the darkness around me. It was a beautiful scene that I was watching unfold in my mind's eye. I could have stayed there a lot longer to watch this show. When I started painting the coloured explosions came bursting forward and just at the end, I could see an eye looking out at me and straight into the core of my being. What does it see that I don't at this point in time? Or maybe it is showing me that 'I can see' what I want, when I want. I loved this one. I enjoyed the colours and the freedom of these creative explosions.

My Message:

When your body and mind are at ease, it is the most wonderful feeling ever. You are not aware of your body or even what you are thinking. This is what being and feeling 'at ease' means. It is a freedom of movement, no aches, no stiffness, and no pain. Your mind is open, your brain is in gear, and you have a greater clarity, better concentration and motivation to achieve.

My Experience:

As I began to paint, using brushes this time; I started in the centre of the large sunflower using a light blue colour, gradually bringing in orange and red and mixing the colour on each petal. I finished one petal before moving on to the next one, and worked my way around. I was so focused and concentrated intensely on what I was doing that I didn't notice my body aching. That was brought to my attention when I stepped back to look at how the painting was progressing. That was when I decided to do another sunflower.

Again I got lost in the process of the painting and spent a good deal of time enjoying the colours and mixing and playing with the paint as the sunflower emerged. I had so much fun with this and I found my body was so much 'at ease' going through this process.

Coming Home - *P

My Message:

When you think of your home and what it means to you, is it where you find security, peace, joy and laughter? Home is where the heart is. Is your heart there or where is it? Your home is primarily your body. Are you happy in yours? What can you do to improve it?

My Experience:

I used paste with the colours and had a great time mixing the colours on the paper, blending it a piece at a time and watching what was emerging as I worked through the palette. When I saw the pathway, I had a sense of it leading me into a special place of security and tranquility. The trees on the left began to appear and the trees on the right followed but I felt they needed to be obscured and not fully painted in. Just a suggestion of trees was what I felt was appropriate. I could see the little thatched cottage with a bale of turf stacked up against it and needed to paint this in. When I did I felt a great sense of 'coming home' to my place of peace and serenity. There is the area to the left of the cottage which can be 'whatever'. I can imagine different things when I use this painting as a meditation.

My Message:

When you look at the golden opportunities that present themselves to you, what do you do? Do you grasp them with open arms or do o wait to analyse it too much and then the moment is gone. Procrastination can rob us of what is waiting to enhance our life. What inspires you to grow? Use this painting so sit and allow your inspiration to flood to you and inspire you.

My Experience:

In my meditation, before this painting, I could see a great big flower head with a river of gold flowing from the centre. It looked amazing. I could see it so clearly and I had a great sense of wellbeing and a contented feeling flooded through my body as watched the golden essence flowing easily towards me. It overflowed and spread this essence outwards. I got the sense that this is how I could feel when I link into this golden orifice. I wondered what would happen if I could paint such an image and how it would make me feel. I really liked this experience as I painted the flower head. I needed to surround each petal in gold for protection, and also the golden essence flowing from the centre.

Rainbow Dance - *P

My Message:

All the colours of the rainbow exist in nature and surround us when we look for them. When we bring these colours into our lives they can be extremely uplifting. Wearing certain colours will also have an effect on your body and your mood. They can either drain you or energise you. See the colours of the rainbow dancing and reflecting. It can balance and harmonise. Use them to your advantage.

My Experience:

I used both hands simultaneously and applied paste first so that it would be easier to apply. Using both hands at the same time activates both sides of the brain and has a calming effect. I was agitated to begin with. As I started with yellow, I kept using the movement up and out, over and over again. I eventually brought in the red, green and blue, mixing them in with the yellow. I began to feel better and more centered. I wanted to reflect these colours as if they were exploding on a horizon. I wanted to have a very clear centre moving upwards. It looks like a person standing and being supported on each side. Fully supported and that support is reflected, mirroring what is there.

Sea Heaven - *P

My Message:

Immerse yourself in this sea heaven to feel the calmness and tranquility seep into the core of your being. Imagine feeling this really warm water covering you from head to toe and washing away the negatives of the day. It can leave you feeling refreshed, complete and ready to take on a brand new day.

My Experience:

Using the paste and choosing light colours I mixed them around and around until these shapes started to appear and I got lost in the detail as it unfurled. Initially I thought that these were turning into flower heads but as the snakes and lobsters appeared I realised that it was a sea painting. It had a very calming effect on me as it came to a conclusion. It represents a cleansing and tranquil place, with never ending movement.

Reflective Peace:- *P

My Message:

Your mind is the conductor of your body. When you think of a time in your life that you really enjoyed and had a good time, your body responds and you can link directly into that feeling just by remembering the incident. Reflect the good times back into your life and uplift your mood as you do so. This will attract more positive energy towards you.

My Experience:

It was nearing the end of the day when I started this painting. I used a lot of paste and very little colour. There is such a great feeling when using my hands with the colours and paste. It allowed me to really be part of the painting and fully 'in touch' with the mood I was in. I felt a great sense of freedom in my body as I painted the sky and the sea. Once I started on the sun I focused on the warmth of the sun penetrating my skin. I remembered times that I had the opportunity to sit in the sun and feel the effect of the heat on my body. Once I did this and related it to the painting, it started to have the desired effect, as if I was sitting and soaking up the sun.

Midday Flight - *P

My Message:

This is a great way of escaping from the restrictions you may be experiencing. You can fly free in your mind, even if your body is not operating at its full potential. Our limitations depend on the openness of your mind and how far you will allow yourself to expand. Look at the painting then close your eyes and allow yourself to soar as high and as far as you wish to go.

My Experience:

This was my last painting of the day and I had been so inspired by the feeling I created during 'Reflective Peace' that wanted to do the same again. Using paste and very little colour this took me approximately fifteen minutes and it was pure joy. I needed to have the sun again, as I wanted to make sure that the experience I had in the previous painting, was not just a once off. And so it was. I could feel the heat of the sun seeping deep down within me as I painted the sun, when I remembered a time in my life that I was lying and absorbing the sun rays. Also, this would have been a time before I had any problems with my body. So, not only could I feel the warmth, I could also feel the freedom that I used to have. I decided to paint in birds in flight as this was what I wanted to feel in my body as I finished the day.

My Message:

Is your eye drawn to the centre of the vortex or are you inclined to go from the outside and travel inwards. What do see as you allow yourself to go with this movement and delve deep down beyond the vortex? What do you need to focus on in your life? Are you paying attention to it or are you ignoring it and wishing it will go away. Pay attention and bring whatever it is to a conclusion. It may be a challenge for you, but it is better to deal with it now and not let it drain your energy anymore.

My Experience:

I loved this one. I loved the colours and the freedom of the movement I experienced when I painted this. I was able to move with ease as I mixed the yellow, orange and red. When I started I had no idea that the painting would be this simple yet energising. Whether it was the colours and the movement combined which made me feel this way as the painting progressed does not matter. What matters is, it changed the way I was feeling.

I painted with paste and my hands and then used a paintbrush to bring the detail out. As I worked with the brush, I became engrossed and focused on the spiraling movement as I placed the dots over and over the piece. It was if the painting was drawing me in over and over again, bringing me to a depth where it felt safe and secure.

Relaxing Tranquility -*P

My Message:

When you look past the rushes and into the background, what can you see? Half close your eyes and see what wants to jump out at you. You can see different things at different times. This is a good one to meditate on, as it can change as you change. Notice how your body wants to relax in the tranquility of the water and the reeds, with the warmth of the sun shining through.

My Experience:

I chose a turquoise colour and a lot of white. Using paste and both hands simultaneously, I used an upward and downward movement and got in touch with the feel of the paint and how it was making me feel as I worked with it. As I continued I could imagine seeing the two sides of a bank with rushes moving upwards. I just needed to paint in the strokes to represent the growth emanating in profusion. I could feel the tranquility in my body as I painted across the water, back and forth, over and over. It had a great calming effect which I could feel inwardly. I finally added the sunlight and left the background obscure.

My Message:

When you look at this painting, what do you sense? Is this a stable and restful sanctuary which keeps you feeling grounded and safe? Or do you have a sense of instability and a feeling of being out on a limb. Filling you with a feeling of insecurity and vulnerability? Or a wonderful feeling of being protected grounded and rock solid in where you are in your life right now?

My Experience:

When I started this I felt quite good. As I continued and it started to materialise I felt quite unsure about the process. I was feeling good, then not too good. When I painted the tree in, I felt really shaky inside. My insides started to tremble and it was not a good experience. I went to lunch and felt quite strange. After lunch, when I looked again at the painting the feeling I had was being 'out on a limb' out of my comfort zone. I felt the urge to paint in some rocks at the base of the tree. When I did I felt more at ease. It was as if the tree needed the support of the rocks to stay upright otherwise it could be blown down and into the water. I do not like water, as a child, I had a near drowning experience, and was saved by a lifeguard on duty. This is probably where this feeling is coming from.

Protectors of my Inner Child - *P

My Message:

Do you feel protected within yourself every day or is there something deep down inside of you that make you feel insecure even today. Do you feel / know that there are events in your past that are responsible for you not reaching your full potential in life. Is it holding you back and preventing you moving forward in life. Know that there are protectors there for you. Ask and know that your request will be answered. Believe that this is already done, and notice the change within.

My Experience:

I had painted out on a limb prior to this one, and it had left me feeling very shaky on the inside. As I painted this, I could see these shapes appearing in very dark turquoise colour, which had another physical effect on me. It was such a profound experience for me, but I was feeling quite unsettled as I painted it. I decided to scratch off the dark turquoise with a palette knife and the figures started to lighten.
As they lightened in colour, my body started to feel lighter and better. I painted white and gold over them to lighten them even more, and again, I physically felt more calm and centered. I had this vision of a tiny baby at the bottom which I outlined in white and gold. White connects to spirit, gold is a protection. I felt that these beings were protectors of my 'Inner Child'. I felt so much better when I finished this painting.

My Message:

When you see this softened heart remember that it is there for you too. The only person that can give this gift of a softened heart in motion is you. Be kind to yourself every day. It is with this kindness that you will notice changes. A change of heart is the best gift that you can administer, not only to you but to those around you. Make it a daily gift and notice a daily shift. It is an empowering thing to do for you and those you love.

My Experience:

As I painted this with my hands I felt so light hearted after 'Protectors of my Inner Child'. This painting was free and easy and no effort or concentration was required. When I finished I could see the heart shape and it looked really soft. This showed me that I need to soften my attitude towards myself and lighten up in relation to my situation.

Even though I feel so restricted in my body, it does not need to translate into my mind. My mind can be as free as I choose it to be and nobody, only me, can give me this freedom of choosing to love myself even when I am not fully functioning physically. It is important for me to be softhearted to myself. It will serve me better as I feel I can move forward faster by honouring myself this way.

My Message:

Every now and then it is important to receive a gift from yourself. Whether this is a 'time out' to do an activity that brings you joy. Or to buy an item that will equally bring you pleasure. How often do you do this for yourself? You do it for others, how about doing it for you. Notice how you feel when you do something nice for you.

My Experience:

I chose turquoise and white and used a sponge roller to start this painting. I saw the outline of the vase and painted it out and filled it with flowers. It was a lighthearted painting and that was exactly how my body was feeling. I felt light in my body and good. I added in the light mesh curtain at the end and finished off with a little ribbon. This gave me a sense of giving myself a gift specially wrapped and nicely presented.

For the past few years I have been so focused on my physical inability to do things, I have nearly forgotten how important it is to do good things for me. I felt good when I stood back to look at the end result and the colour is one of my favourites.

Birthing of Past Fears - *P

My Message:
What fears do you carry with you? Have you buried your fears deep down within? Or do you live in fear every day? We can learn to move through life holding on to fears. But we end up existing rather than living. It takes energy to hold on to fears. This energy could be used more wisely. It is similar to an investment. We can invest energy wisely or unwisely. Holding fears and living with them is an un-healthy investment. We need to let them go and no longer be a slave to them. When we allow this freedom to happen, we can move mountains within ourselves and those energy blocks can simply melt away.

My Experience:

In my meditation I could see this skull moving towards me, and I felt a great hardness in the pit of my stomach. It was rock solid and it felt like a very heavy weight inside of me. As my meditation progressed, I felt as though my body was allowing this stone weight to pass outside of me. It was as if I was giving birth to it. I needed to paint it out and see what happened. This large skull appeared and then I could see more skulls in the distance. This was a really strange experience, and it had quite an effect on my physical body. I felt so much better when I was finished and it was a great release. The physical feeling was tremendous. I had allowed this hardness and stone weight feeling that I had been carrying to dissipate as I painted.

"Time" to flow into Stillness (stem the flow) - *P

My Message:

Let the colour flow over you into a stillness that helps to calm the essence of your being. Imagine wading through this warm silky water, as it heats your body to a temperature that fills you with pleasure and joy. Have a sense that the great brick wall is a security surrounding you and is there for your protection and wellbeing.

My Experience:

This was the last painting of this workshop and I had a wonderful few days with great messages coming through in my paintings. As I painted the white and blue together it felt like a rush of this waterfall dropping down into a stillness of calm. It felt really good and then I felt the need to paint the brick wall to contain the waterfall to stem the flow. There was a great calmness in the water, as I felt a great calmness in my body. It was a wonderful way to end the workshop with this sense of achievement and a sense of contentment as well.

Heart Centre – Staying Calm & Focused - *P

My Message:

When you look at this painting, does the colour sit well with you or does it stir up emotions. Are you able to stay calm and focused when all around is moving at an incredible pace. Can you detach yourself from the disruption and achieve what you need to. Focusing on the negative will bring keep you in the 'Stinking Thinking' regime. While honing in on the positive, staying calm and focused, will allow you to 'Blossom and Grow'. You can achieve more, do more and it will make you feel better.

My Experience:

I chose a great deal of colours before I started painting, and I used paste and my hands. The colours flowed about in a circle and it seemed like a rush of colours swirling and twirling in a madness that seemed out of control. Yet there was this heart shape beginning to emerge in a very light colour in the centre. Light green, yellow and white, quite different to the outside darkness and tone.
I outlined the heart centre in red, so that it would stand out in the frenzy. It reminded me of remaining calm and staying focused even though there is so much disruption around. I felt really good at the end and I could recognise the difference between the calmness in my heart centre, even though my body is going through the physical turmoil.

My Message:

What have you done recently for fun? Is it time for you to organize a daily/weekly/monthly event to have some fun, relax and play? When you have a balance in your life you will be more productive. Taking the time will help you to reap the rewards that you deserve. Work rest and play, everything in moderation is a great way forward.

My Experience:

I started with the paste and light colours turquoise and white, and swirled the paint back and forth like a rainbow going over and back. When I brought the yellow in it started a horizon line with the footpath emerging. The little thatched cottage emerged again with the turf stack at the side and a fire billowing smoke into the air. Again I find myself feeling very much 'at home' with this painting. I got so lost in it as the water and pier appeared. It reminded me of all the boating I used to do with the family years ago. We had so much fun playing with the children and enjoying ourselfes as a family unit. This inspired me to put in a little fishing boat. I realise that I have set aside no relaxing or leisure time to have fun and play in the past number of years. I need to factor this in for the family's sake as well as for mine. I miss it so much, and it is extremely hard to do when my physical body is so challenged.

Twilight Forest - *L

My Message:

Come into the forest. Walk your way into the twilight zone where you can conjure up your dream. See it in your mind's eye, sense it as if you have already achieved and captured it, as you feel this sensation filling your mind and body. Notice how good it is to achieve what you wish for. There are no limitations to where your mind and imagination can bring you. No boundaries or borders. When you continue to 'dream your dream' it can become your reality. When you believe it, you can achieve it.

My Experience:

I chose the orange and red and massaged the colour on the paper, feeling an energizing effect as it moved easily and effortlessly. While the paint was still wet I scratched off the wet paint to symbolize the branches of the trees. It gave an eerie and twilight look. I painted in the trees and then I scratched out the roadway. Then I painted in the rocks in the foreground. The moon was the last to be painted in. I loved painting it and I loved the end result. It looks as though you could take a walk in there and discover little hideaways all over this forest. This was a great experience, with a great feeling in my body when I was finished.

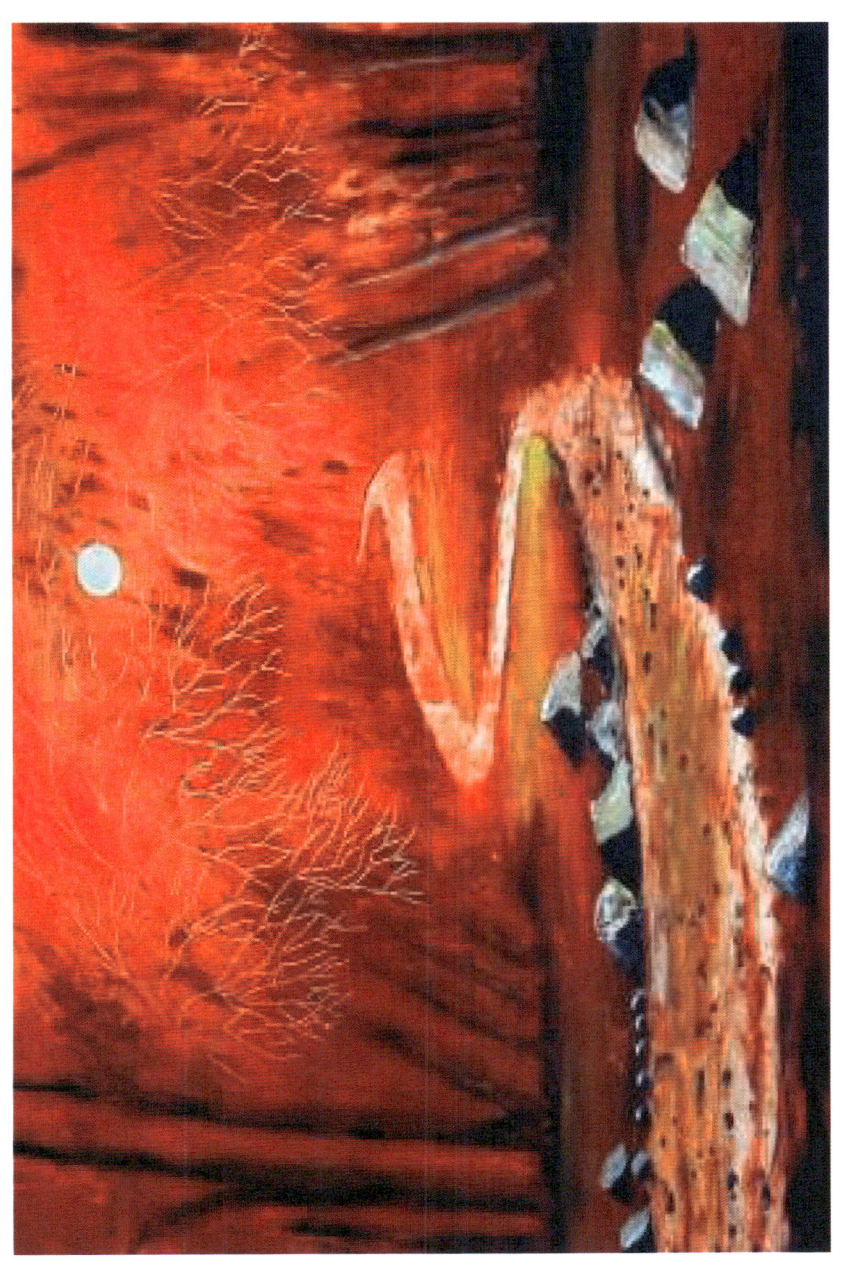

Fireworks – Letting Go - *L

My Message:
What lights your fire? When you look at this, 'letting go' what does it stir up for you? Where do you feel this in your body? Do you feel it in your head, heart, stomach or back? Just notice where it is and what does it feel like? What memories does it bring up for you? Have you dealt with this in the past? If you have some letting go to do, allow it to happen. See the memory in your 'mind' and watch it explode into smithereens. Your mind is so powerful that it can do that for you, if you want it too. Then notice the lightness in your body and mind.

My Experience:

I really let go when I was painting this. There was no stopping me. I felt as though I was on fire and needed to explode. It was probably why I chose the red to begin with. I basically used the tips of my fingers and felt as though I could barely touch the paper. I chose blue then to tone it down a little, but even at that, it still had the 'on fire' effect. I was in a mad rush to do this. It felt crazy, yet good at the same time. When I started with the yellow I seemed to slow down a bit, just like a calming effect after the mad start. When I stood back and viewed the end result, I realised that I needed to lash this out because this was how I was feeling before I started painting. Now that it was out on the paper, I physically felt a good deal better.

My Message:

When you work methodically through a project, it helps to keep you focused and it takes your mind away from what your body and mind is demanding. Working with colour in this way can literally set you free from these demands as your attention is drawn away as you enjoy the process of laying the changing shapes on the paper. Take the time to enjoy a masterpiece of your own and use it for your daily meditation

My Experience:

Working with brushes I started with the blue flower on the left and used one brush stroke per petal to begin with. I worked my way around the flower and moved to the red one on the top. I was feeling quite upset before I started painting and as I continued I was deep in the process and got really lost in it.
I wasn't concerned that these flowers do not represent anything growing naturally, but that did not even enter my head. It is not about perfection it is about expressing what I was feeling at the time. By the time I was getting to the stage of painting in the centres I was feeling a great deal better and was looking forward to completing it. I became more relaxed the longer I was working on floral gift. The painting process and what it delivers, is the real gift. I finished with a light wash of red mixed with a lot of water.

My Message:

What do you see and feel when you look at this painting. Do you feel unbalanced or balanced? What does this represent to you? Does it remind you of when you are going around in circles and getting nowhere? When you have a day like that it is important to stop and centre yourself. Visualise the pyramid shape and feel the strength of such a foundation deep down within you. Place this visual of the pyramid at your naval and notice how much stronger you feel after this exercise.

My Experience:

I started this one with black, and using the brush, I just let the brush take on a life of its own. It was interesting to see what transformed as I relaxed more into the process. I felt like a child colouring in and having fun. This was an interesting exercise. It made me laugh at the shape that was taking place. It reminded me of a clown messing about and falling around as he twists and turns. Right in the centre is a triangular shape. This was the last piece of the puzzle. For me this represents the solid foundation at the centre of my being. It needs to be as solid as the pyramids that have stood the test of time for centuries, long lasting and sturdy. The colours represent the colours of the chakras in balance.

Releasing the Transformation - *L

My Message:
A transformation is looking to come forward for you. Understand that when you are going with the flow of life and understanding that connection and awareness is a key to this development. Become still in the present, be willing to let go of the past and notice what can transpire. If you want to find the meaning in the transformation, pay attention to the moment, and it's in the moment that you find the rewards.

My Experience:

I started in the left hand corner mixing red, black and blue as I moved from left to right. Then I moved down the right hand side and the figure in black started to emerge. It looked weird but it also gave me a sense of reverence at the same time.
This yellow light in the centre emanated right up into the top where I saw a spirit shape flying overhead. This spirit guide always presents itself when there is something major about to change in my life. It has become a pattern that I have recognised and welcome. The change is always for the best, although at the time it may not feel like that.
I have learnt that sometimes an uncertain time or an unpleasant situation usually turns out to be a blessing in disguise. When I see this spirit guide appearing in my paintings, I trust that it is bringing a life changing event or opportunity, so that I can blossom and grow.
Then I painted the figure on the left, which seemed to have a lot of light emanating out of his back. It looked as if I am going to need some protection for what has to come. I am trusting that because my spirit guide is present, all will be okay. I need to trust it now.

Doorway to Freedom – light, love, harmony & contentment - *P

My Message:

Your freedom is there for you to claim it when you need it. Freedom starts in your mind and once there it flows to your body effortlessly. What would you like to see and feel in your life as you open this door to your freedom? Write it down and visualise it so that you can create it and bring it closer to you.

My Experience:

I started with a lot of light green and as my hand moved from left to right, it created this archway effect. It continued in this way until I realised that there was the opportunity and inspiration to create this into a doorway. I used red paint for this and I felt the urge to finish this painting really fast and not linger during it. There was an excitement within me to 'get it done'. I loved the sense of excitement, as I haven't felt this emotion in a long time. It was a great feeling. When the doorway was painted I wanted to put some stained glass at the top of this door, and when I did, I could see the heart shape appear. I then put a red heart shape container at the left hand side of the door. At the end I had a sense of Lightness, Love, Harmony and Contentment in my body.

My Message:

Think about the things in your life that you need to separate yourself from. What is holding you back from progressing forward? When you have an opportunity for good things to happen i.e., holidays planned, and inevitably something goes wrong either before, during or after to spoil the 'good time' you could have had. Is this a continuing trend that you experience?

My Experience:

I do not know what I am attracting into my life right now, whatever it is I do not like it. I am not long home from a couple of days in the hospital having broken my elbow and smashed my face on the ground. What do I need to 'face' now and why am I given another 'timeout'? Because I broke my right arm, I have to paint this with my left hand. I feel this is me standing in the middle of the road and making a very strong statement "**Stop, I have had enough. I am no longer attracting negative energy destroying my progress and healing**" These men in black, who are trying to reach representations of myself on the left, are being stopped in their tracks by me. I am determined to succeed in a 'final separation' from disasters. My spirit guide is here again to protect me for what is to come. When this spirit guide shows up there is a major change coming, I claim a positive outcome.

Flight, Cunning, Wisdom, Strength, Lightness

My Message:

These land and air animals are very strong and also quite nimble. Each animal has their own qualities to bring to you, for you to claim from them. Connect to each one and sense what you would gain from them, if you could converse with them, what would you say? What wisdom would you gain from them?

My Experience:

I took reds and yellows and some brown and blended the whole background together it was quite difficult as I was doing this with my left hand. When I stood back to look at what wanted to come forward I saw the birds head at the top left and the fox head on the top right hand side. The owl head was right there in the centre and I started painting him in and as I was doing this I could see the horses head on the left as well. I was having a great time painting this (although in a lot of pain – right elbow broken) I was experiencing a great excitement with the animals that were presenting themselves. It took me all I had to contain this excitement, but this was helping me to keep my mind off the pain I was in. I could see two more horses and a squirrel on the bottom right. This was brilliant to paint. I had a great sense of achievement and satisfaction when I stood back to see the end result. Power animals with swiftness and agility, I can certainly do with these qualities in my current situation, so I am claiming these powers as my own, and bringing them into my body and mind.

Walkway - *P

My Message:
When things go pearshaped for you, you may feel devastated and wonder why is this happening? There is a reason for everything. For every action there is an equal and opposite re-action. "When one door of opportunity closes, another one opens, but sometimes we are so busy looking at the closed door, that we do not see the new door that has been opened for us". ***Helen Keller***

My Experience:
My trees appear again, which shows me that I am grounded and rock steady, because trees represent this feeling to me. This is what the painting process is showing me, but my body does not feel like this at present. I feel battered, bruised, face is stitched and arm in a sling, but, I am trusting what is happening in the painting and feel that there is **major** change occuring.

In the past, I would have felt sorry for myself after having my accident, but I know that this has happened for a reason and I need to know what this is for me. This time, I am going with the flow and decided to paint to understand **why** I need to stop and take the time I need to recover. I need to meditate to see what wants to reveal itself.

When I look into 'walkway' there is a lot of mystery between the trees. I can see a lot of different things in there. What they are and what they represent, I do not know. I need to let things unfold in their own time. I have plenty of that now as I am confined until my body heals. I am so grateful to have Heart Art 'Magic' so I can express my frustration and let the message unfold. I am looking forward to hearing/seeing/and feeling it.

Dialogue Nomed & ME - *P

My Message: If this Demon, represented the demons that you have been harbouring within you. What bugs you? What ticks you off? Know what this is and have a conversation with this 'demon' and ask what does it want from you, what purpose is it serving? Take a pen and paper and write down your questions and the answers you receive. Do it instantly and don't delay with the answers. Be instinctive and let it flow. You will be amazed at what can be revealed to you.

My Experience:
When I looked at this painting I could see this Demon which I christened ooo as I didn't want to give it any power by giving it a name. I started a dialogue with it and asked "why are you here facing me"? This painting had an ENORMOUS effect on me and a huge impact as a result of the dialogue that I had with it. This was a turning point in my ability to move forward to improve my physical ability to recover. The thought of having this 'chat' with this demon was quite disturbing for me and I felt it was very hard to do. I started the dialogue on the defensive but there was a transformation during the dialogue process.

The result was AMAZING. I had viewed this as a Demon there to taunt me, what transpired was a 'being' sent to protect me. It allowed me to 'let go' of the deep painful sorrow, and more especially the guilt that I carried with me from the age of eight. I called this 'being' Nomed = demon spelt backwards. "Nomed I accept your extended hand as a gesture of future friendship and Positive Powerful Energy Source" I felt my shoulders have sunk and relaxed. My tears of sorrow have stopped. My tears of Joy may continue for a while, as I take in my NEW found Peace and Contentment that I can allow to fulfill me as I breathe. I feel with this revelation that I can truly live in the present moment and be free to be me. At last!!!

My message:

When you see this painting, know that you have lifted and shifted layers of negative energy from within. Now it is time to smile and move with ease. Enjoy the feeling and sense the joy that this brings to you now. Even when you are experiencing challenging times, keep looking at Smiles and Styles to encourage you to keep positive and continue moving forward.

My Experience:

I feel so much more at ease now than I have ever felt in my 'Lifetime'. The previous paintings; 'Final Separation' cutting the past away, and finally. 'Flight, Cunning, Wisdom, Strength, Lightness', I received these qualities for what was to come. 'Walkway' was protection for a major change. 'Nomed & Me', the dialogue that eventually set me free from my guilt and grief. Smiles & Styles when I painted this I felt more focused. I enjoyed the background colours purple and blue and they mixed and swirled around and around. The frock shape in the centre was the first to emerge. The other figures followed and then the face at the top was the last to appear. I see a happy, smiling, and contented look. I feel a great sense of movement when I look at this picture. Again this painting took a few days to do. What I have noticed is I am more focused when I start a project; I am bringing it to a conclusion. It is liberating and freeing. I don't feel bogged down. I feel light, free and happy (even with my broken arm).

Bird Of Paradise - *L

My Message:

When you look at this bird of paradise, are you living in your own paradise at present? View this painting as a means for you to claim what you want to bring into your life. If you could paint your own perfect place, picture it in your mind and hold that image there and add to it as time goes along. Enjoy this process and enjoy your outcome.

My Experience:

This really was a paradise experience. I felt as though I was in paradise when I was painting this. The colours were the hint in naming this bird of paradise. My body feels light and free. I am physically, emotionally, mentally and spiritually healed for the first time that I can remember. It is so liberating and freeing to feel this way.
I know that I have missed out for the majority of my lifetime, but better late than never. I am so grateful for my health and happiness and am still reeling from my discovery from my last set of paintings. I found it such a profound revelation and it was so awe inspiring.
I am looking forward to my future, as I know I can have a hand in designing my outcome. I will continue to build on what I have learnt in my journey of discovery. My thinking will remain positive and grow stronger as time passes.

My Message:

Are you going with the flow in life, or are you swimming against it the tide? A little adjustment on how you view where you are can just flip the situation, right back into the right direction. Your perception may need to be tweaked just a little or maybe a lot, only you can know what is needed. If you think you can, you will. If you think you can't, you're right. Make the right choice and go with the flow, it is easier in the long run.

My Experience:

The background on this was light and airy and it was such a pleasure as I worked easily and effortlessly. I saw the orange fish first and instantly knew that this was going to be an underwater scene. The rest of the menagerie cropped up one by one. I enjoyed taking my time and choosing the colours as I went along. It flowed really well and each fish was a pleasure to paint. It was relaxing and uplifting.
This showed me that when I am in a relaxed and focused mood, I can go with the flow of life more easily, than if I am tense. It makes more sense for me to connect to my 'higher self' before I do a task and then I work smarter, I also noticed that I feel more alert, have greater clarity and I and am more effective and efficient.

RISK MORE THAN OTHERS THINK IS SAFE.

DREAM MORE THAN OTHERS THINK IS PRACTICAL.

CARE MORE THAN OTHERS THINK IS WISE.

DESIRE MORE THAN OTHERS THINK IS POSSIBLE......

..... AND THE UNIVERSE IS YOURS.

My Message:

Transcending into calmness can help you to move forwards faster in life. Even though you may feel that taking time to stop and reflect is too time consuming, it actually has the opposite effect. It is an investment in time that gives a good return. By taking the 'time' to stop and think, it frees up the clutter in your brain. You can prioritise effectively, think clearly, do a great job and remain focused till you have it completed. This will make you will feel great.

My Experience:

This was a great. I loved the touch of the paint on my hands as it glided over the paper. The lightness of the colour reflected my mood as the trees disappeared into infinity.
This could be a roadway or a river; it is really hard to tell. It is whatever I want it to be. I can change it to suit how I feel whenever I look at it. The same way that I can change my mood to be whatever I want it to be, just by changing my thinking. I felt I was transcending into a calmness that I had created in a few minutes.
When the painting was still wet I used a palette knife to scrape out the bark of the tree trunks and the branches. Likewise in life, removing things can just be as effective as adding something in or replacing things.

My Message:
Do not hold guilt or grief in your body/mind for too long. Over time, it can have a devastating effect. The person you are grieving, would not like to know that you are suffering. Do something positive in their memory instead.

My Experience:
In 2000, when I was confined to my bed I composed this poem: **Forgiveness for Freedom**
I forgive myself for all the times I did not like myself,
I forgive myself for all the times I did not love myself,
I forgive myself for ever hurting anyone, I forgive anyone for ever hurting me.
I forgive myself, and them, in order to choose FREEDOM.
Since I was eight years old, I have carried the guilt and the grief for Tony's death. Today I forgive myself for the torment that I caused myself and my family especially my parents. When I look at my eight year old granddaughter, it reminds me how simple and uncomplicated life is for her in her innocence. And that is what an eight year old is supposed to be, innocent with no worries and cares to consider. It makes me stop and think that although I felt I knew (at the time of Tony's accident) that I could have avoided it happening, I know now, as an adult, that there was nothing I could do to prevent it.
I thought that I had forgiven myself over and over again, but this form of releasing through painting has allowed the FINAL threads of guilt and grief to dissolve gently and effectively. As I continue to paint using my Heart Art 'Magic' system, the release continues to happen and I do not have to think about. It is automatic. It shows up in the paintings as revelations to behold.

Fearless – Freedom from Fear - *L

My Message:

We can be disabled by fear, and it comes in all sorts of different ways for different people. It can be debilitating and can hold you back from operating at your full potential. Fears and Phobias are a major factor in today's society. This way of working with meditation and painting can help release the fears, especially if they are very deep rooted and embedded in the core of your being. You can use Heart Art 'Magic' to work your way to freedom.

My Experience:

As usual I had no idea what was to come as this painting started. I chose the blue and black and mixed them on the paper with the paste. The first shape I saw appearing was the Saber Toothed Tiger, which is now extinct. Just like the fear I used to carry, is gone for good. The Black Panther was there next, I just needed to outline his eyes, nose and mouth. There are other animals in there that I can see, but did not have to outline them or bring them out. Can you see any?
All the other animals came forward one by one as I progressed through the painting. The snake was interesting as I enjoyed giving him a textured skin. I realised during the past few months that the fears that once haunted me, are now laid to rest, and it is a liberating experience to feel so light and free. I am extremely grateful for this feeling and will always be so.

A Love Heart Gift to Myself - *P

My Message:

Do you need to give yourself a gift of some kind? Perhaps you have been too hard on yourself lately. It is really important to like and love yourself. When you do, you will feel better, be better and get better results in your life. When you have a good relationship with yourself, the relationships that you have with others will flourish and grow. Do yourself and others a favour and give yourself this gift. When you 'want to change then change to love'.

My Experience:

When I saw the heart shape appearing, it was a gentle reminder for me to keep the 'love flow' growing within me. It took me a long time to learn that the person I need to respect and love first, is myself.

I used to think that this would be selfish, but I know now that it is not. It allows me to be self FULL. When I am self full, with love and energy, then, that energy and love is overflowing. The people nearest and dearest to me receive that overflow. It is important that I maintain the love heart gift to myself always; this painting is a reminder for me to do so. I do this in respect of others and also for my highest good and will. I feel blessed with this message.

Rock Steady Balance – A Cut Thru – Break-Thru - *L

My Message:

Notice how big the pyramid is in relation to the diamonds and circles. How rock steady are you in everyday life? The pyramid is your foundation for stability. Notice whatever is blocking you, and know that you can cut through it with the diamond, which is one of the hardest rock and cutting tool on the planet. Your circle of life continues to spiral in a positive fashion when you use the stability of the pyramid and the sharpness of the diamond to help you to follow your dream. Go with it and enjoy your journey.

My Experience:

I chose my favourite turquoise to start with and completed the background. I could see the very definite pyramid shape which I outlined with a darker blue. Then I saw some diamond shapes and circles with tails. I could feel a tremendous stability with the painting of the pyramid. Rock Steady Balance, is unshakable and ultimately stable. It is a feeling that I am claiming for myself and for my future. The best cutting tool is a diamond. I know that I have made a cut thru-break thru in my life and I intend to live life to the fullest. There is so much I want to achieve, and helping others to achieve as well, is really important to me.

Blue Haven - *L

My Message:

Reach into the blueness of the heart shaped haven. Feel the protection of the mountains reaching up into the sky. The heat of the sun, shining brighter as it glows on the water. See this as your beautiful peaceful place of tranquility and a haven to relax in. You can find the answers to some questions that you have been asking lately. Imagine sitting in the middle of this haven and asking for what you want. See, feel and know that you have it.

My experience:

This experience was wonderful. The painting was done in about twenty minutes. There was no hesitation to choosing the colours or starting the process. I was feeling extremely comfortable. My body is pain-free and relaxed. I am so happy to be here today even though I struggled with the decision to come to the workshop. I had not got the dates in the diary. I have been really busy lately keeping to an exercise regime and program which is helping me enormously.

I missed the last workshop because I was unable to stand, sit or walk without pain, yet again. It was another 'time for reflection' on what was happening, and the result of my meditation was to bring Heart Art 'Magic' to the general public as a healing method. I needed to share the value of this work and help others just as I have been helped over the past number of years. This has now become part of my mission.

Extraction - *P

My Message:

If you have something that is bugging you and acting as a thorn in your side, what do you want to do? Leave it fester or have it removed? When you leave it, it will create a problem. When you address it, although that may not be easy, it can open up new possibilities and a new beginning. Have courage and go for it. The only person that can extract it is you. Is this what you would like to do, or can do?

My Experience:

As I painted this, I felt the urge to rush into it and get it done quickly. I worked with brushes and used strokes running in the same direction. I worked furiously to get it finished. I do not know why I needed to rush it, but it was extremely urgent for me to do so as quickly as possible. As I outlined the shape with brown I could get the sense of this representing a wooden mallet with splintered edges.

It was as if this was the greatest 'thorn in my side' and now it was being extracted straight out of my body. It was a great feeling of releasing, and then it felt as though there was a great void waiting to be filled. There was a wonderful relief when I was finished the painting. I felt great. I am totally pain free and have great movement and a freedom in my body. I feel so grateful for this.

Filling the Void - *P

My Message:

What qualities would you like to increase within yourself? If you could do this in an instant what would you wish for? Wonderful feelings like contentment, peace, joy, high self-esteem, motivation, confidence etc. How would you feel when you have instilled these qualities of your choice? Imagine how powerful you could be by doing this in your mind and let it be absorbed into your body. Remember what you think about you bring about. Doing this constantly is a great way to start your day and eventually it becomes habitual and automatic.

My Experience:

I used big brushes and red and yellow paint. I started painting circles and they just flowed out one after the other. The big brushes made an easy job of this as I continued. It had a beautiful feeling to it. I then felt the urge to surround each one with gold for protection. The need to protect these is paramount for my future wellbeing. This was an instinctual feeling.

When I was coming to the end, I wanted to cover the entire clump of new cells with gold once again. That was exactly what this painting represented. A nucleus of new cells filling the void left by the major extraction from the previous painting.

Another start - *L

My Message:

If you could have a new start, what would you wish it to be? What do you 'need' to change or what would you 'like' to change. If you are struggling in any area in your life, think about this now, and if you could change things, what outcome would you wish for? How would your choices transform your situation to become a solution for you?

My Experience:

I started by dipping my fingers in the yellow and red and green and made this big circle which moved out to the sides. I took a long time doing this action before I got a sense of what was happening. There was a great flow to this and it felt as though I could go on and on.
I then took the big brushes again and started making the circles in the centre, starting with the red ones and then the yellow ones. I had no idea at the time, why I still wanted to paint these little circles again. But then I began to see the relationship of the nucleus of new cells, this time multiplying over and over, as if they were in utero with the fallopian tubes moving out to the sides. With another new beginning comes another new start.
For some reason I was still feeling really excited while I was painting during this workshop? Maybe it is because my body is so much at ease and I am feeling great. I just know that it is a great feeling that my body is not bringing my attention to any specific part that is screaming for attention. I feel free!!!

Birthing - *P

My message:

Look at the colours and the shape and notice how you feel when you absorb what you see? Does it energise you or does it drain you? Or maybe you do not feel a connection to it at all. If you had the chance to re- live your life, what would you be doing now? How would that choice make you feel? We can be the masters of our own destiny or we can drift along aimlessly.

My experience:

I thoroughly enjoyed this painting. I started with outlining the shape, again using the big brushes, and I felt a great connection to it instantly. I chose the yellows and reds and just mixed them together as I went along. I was blown away by the strength of the colours and the shape which had a profound effect on me. When I looked at it I felt as though it was a birthing.

The circle at the bottom representing a baby's head exiting from the womb, and bringing a new life into the world and the little red head at the top, not able to go the full distance. It reminded me of the 'Vibration of Life' painting which showed my twin sharing the womb with me initially, but not reaching full term.

Since 'Vibration of Life' emerged, I have never felt the loneliness that I grew up with. I have had a complete fulfillment in myself and am very happy in my own space. I feel my twin in Spirit and know that she is there helping me whenever I need direction or solutions. I am grateful for her Spiritual presence and assistance.

New Beginnings - A wiser head on young shoulders - *P

My Message:

A newborn brings so much joy and softness; it brings a new personality with new qualities. A newborn requires special attention and great care is needed to nurture it every couple of hours of everyday of every week, month and year. It needs constant caring until it becomes independent and can take on a direction of its own. When you start a new direction remember the newborn and what its needs are. Give yourself the same care and attention during your new nurturing period.

My Experience:

I really, really felt the urge and I mean a great urge (Big Time) to paint a newborn baby. The face was serene and not very 'newborn' looking. It seemed that this head seemed to be older and wiser. A beginning of a new life, putting 'an old head on young shoulders', which brings wisdom that, is so special and unique. I feel I am embarking on a new path with a renewed energy. This is the most wonderful feeling ever. I have never been happier than I am right now at any of the workshops I attended. I have freedom of movement. I am centered and focused. I feel fantastic. And most of all I am extremely grateful for the messages in the paintings that are flooding out. It is an incredible journey and a wonderful way of discovering what wants to come forward and be revealed. A picture paints a thousand words. This is so true.

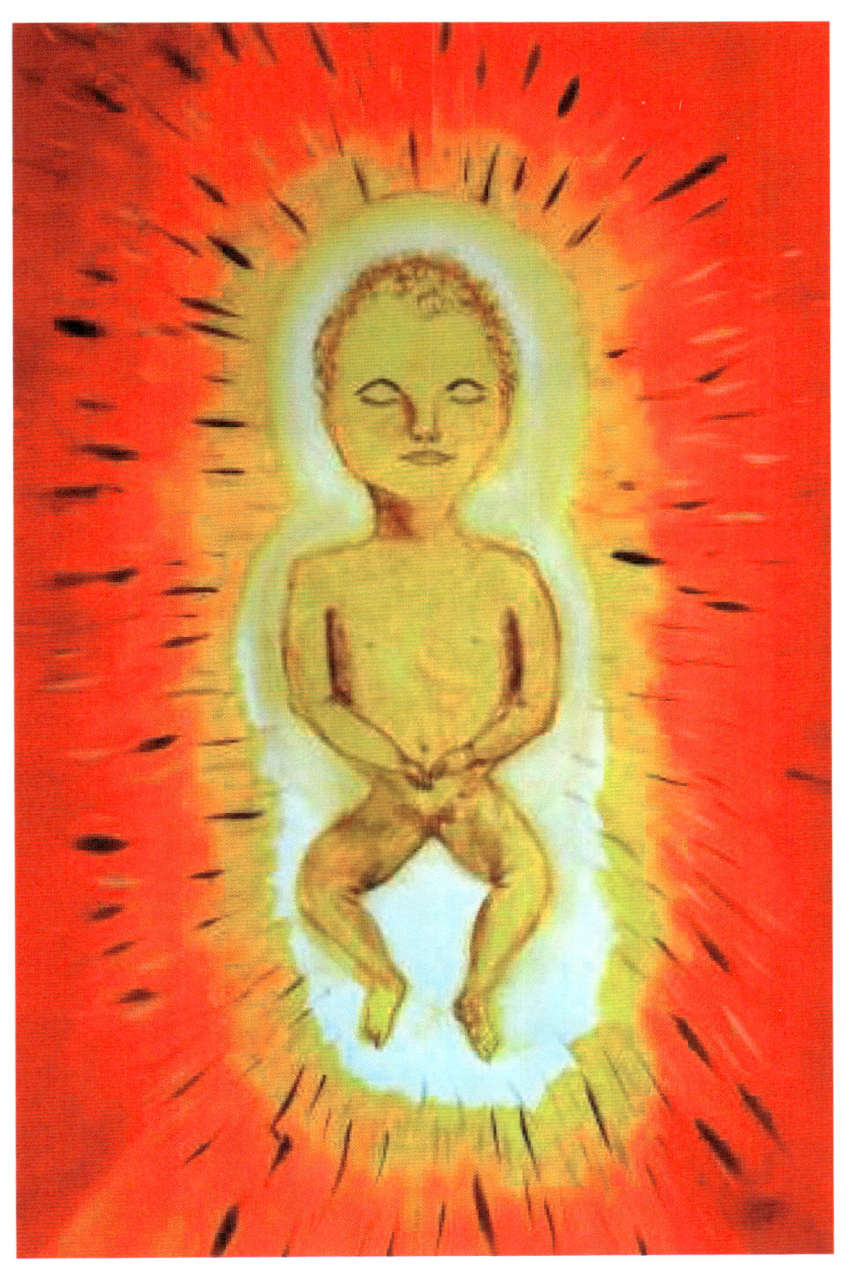

Time for Play - *P

My Message:

It is important to make time for play, because when you do, it makes the rest of your day feel balanced and equal. When you do this, your day is more structured and you will get more things done. Quality is much better than quantity. Play releases endorphins into your body and it energises you. You will save time in your day by making time for play.

My Experience:

This was a pure pleasure to paint. I felt like a child doing a fairytale painting. I first saw the big birds head and the enormous eye watching. The eye was so definite in comparison to the rest of the bird which seems translucent and that is the way I needed to paint this bird. It is like a protector in the background watching and protecting. Then I painted the flowers and I saw the little bird standing in the middle of a branch. He looked so alone and vulnerable and when I stood back to have a better view of the painting I could see the shape of the other bird flying upwards to join him.
This wonderful 'being' of energetic protection is watching down over them, making sure that they are safe in their play.
Taking the time for play is extremely important to get the work life balance correct. The one thing I have learnt on this journey is that if I do not take the 'timeout', it will be done for me. I prefer it to be my choice from here on in.

My Message:

It's important to ask for help, make a connection on a daily basis. When you ask, and believe, you will receive. It is important that you think about what you want. Therefore it is important to ask for something that is good and positive. Ask for things that will energise you or somebody else. You can say it in a prayer, if that is your form of asking. You can ask for guidance. The energy is there for us to draw on, whenever we need to.

My Experience:

There was a great urgency for me to use the same colours as the last painting "Time for Play". I cannot explain why, but I just went with the feeling anyway. These beings represent guides to me. Every now and again they show up in my paintings, and it is as though they are giving me the guidance I need to move forward in life. I also feel that they are letting me know that they are there for me whenever I need to call them in. It is a wonderful feeling to know that we are never on our own and we have an energy that will work with us. But they will only do that, when and if we ask. So it is important to do that, and request positive things that will fuel you to be the best that you can be.

Imbalance – Keep Balance Always - *P

My message:

It is extremely important to make sure that you take the time out for a balanced lifestyle. You will achieve more in your day. You will feel better and function better as well. Take the time to plan every week. Make a commitment to yourself to do what is right for you to have a carefree happy lifestyle. The better the balance, the better your life will be. It makes sense to put a balance in place, because if you don't, you won't. You can pay the price for it later. Don't go sailing through life without a sail and a rudder on your boat, otherwise you will be going around in circles and getting nowhere.

My Experience:

I had no idea what this painting meant as it progressed. I enjoyed doing it and I liked the colours. When I anaylised it at the end, it reminded me of a weighing scales being out of balance. Look at the two squares, they are totally unbalanced. And then I could relate the bends and turns that I saw in this painting, with my body being doubled over and out of kilter.
If I do not take the care to get the proper balance right, in my daily life, then I will only have myself to answer to. That is what happened just a few weeks ago, when I found myself having to take to bed again. I found it hard to stand, walk or sit. The only comfort I could get was lying down. I need a balance in my work, rest and play, every day, for perfect harmony and perfect balance, if I want to keep moving forward.

My Message:

This is another reminder to take some time to connect to your 'higher self' as it can give you a freedom that you never thought possible. It is a wonderful way of knowing that you will be given the correct messages for you to 'be the best that you can be'. Remember to do this daily as it then becomes automatic. A very dear friend always says "mankind needs to be reminded rather than informed". Most times we go with the flow of life. But sometimes we get lost. I am reminding you to stay connected and get the best out of life.

My Experience:

When I saw what was appearing, it was clear to me that I am being reminded again that I need to keep connecting to 'spirit' in order to stay well and safe for everyday living. When I do this, my body will be more comfortable, and my life will be so much easier. I have had a lot of reminders of this message in my paintings. I have had the best few days painting and I feel incredible. I am extremely healthy, pain free, energetic and so grateful to have been introduced to Heart Art 'Magic'. It has been in incredible journey for me. I feel I have completed a full circle of life. I have a freedom now that I have not had in the past number of years. I now live my life in Gratitude every day.

When your eyes, sees your hand do the work of your heart, your circle of life is complete.

Chapter Nine – The door to freedom

All my paintings had a positive effect on me. Even though some of them made me feel ill while I was painting them, it was still a turning point for the better. The last ten paintings in particular were so profound for me. I was blown away with the message that these gave me. I started **with Blue Haven**, which felt as if there was a great protection in this beautiful place.

 Extraction, which felt as though the remnants of grief and guilt were extracted from my subconscious mind. **Filling the Void,** with new positive cells. **Another Start** gave me a new kick start, helping me to make new changes. **Birthing** is this 'new change' deep down within me. **New Beginnings** is a much more relaxed, wiser, empowered and more positive Marian. **Time for Play** is so important that I achieve a good 'work/rest/ play' **life balance. Calling in,** it is important that I call upon my guides for direction on a daily basis. **Imbalance**, when I keep the balance right in my life I will operate at my fullest potential. **Connection is Key**, it is really imperative that I keep the daily connection to Spirit to receive Inspiration.

"One of life's most fulfilling moments occurs in that split second when the familiar is suddenly transformed into the dazzling aura of the profoundly new.... These breakthroughs are too infrequent, more uncommon than common; and we are mired most of the time in the mundane and the trivial.

The shock; what seems mundane and trivial is the very stuff that discovery is made of. The only difference is our perspective, our readiness to put the pieces together in an entirely new way and to see patterns where only shadows appeared just a moment before. – Edward B Lindaman. *Thinking in Future Tense 1978*

It is true that when you are totally engrossed and focused you can function at a higher level of consciousness, and draw upon a stream of enlightenment that you never knew existed. This form of expression is liberating and enjoyable, but not only that, it is a mirroring of your lifetime and can bring about revelations that can amaze you.

It is a wonderful way of truly expressing the potential that you have locked up inside the deepest core of your being, which is attempting to come out into the open. It has helped me to come full circle and has enabled me to put my life into perspective. The messages I received by this way of expression has blown me away with the direction that I have received.

"We begin with a concept of some kind of basic awareness, some kind of basic ability to 'know' or sense' or 'cognise' or 'recognise' that something is happening. This is a fundamental theoretical and experiential given. We do not know scientifically what the ultimate nature of awareness is, but it is our starting point". – Charles T. Tart. *Alternate States of Consciousness. 1975*

I am truly grateful that I have been given this opportunity to express myself in this way as it has given me a true picture of where I am now, and where my journey started and my lifetime in between.

I have had a few challenges in life which had a profound effect on everyday living. Heart Art 'Magic' has opened the doors to freedom for me. It has given me a freedom to **'live in the moment'** and enjoy life to the full.

"Art is a form of supremely delicate awareness... meaning at–oneness, the state of being at one with the object...The picture must all come out of the artist's inside...It is the image that lives in the consciousness, alive like a vision, but unknown. –
D.H. Lawrence

How to get started using Heart Art 'Magic' painting process.

Step 1:

Put the paper up with masking tape. Have your materials all ready.

Step 2:

Relax or Meditate for five to ten minutes minimum. Use relaxing music or no music at all. (See meditation on page 250)

Step 3:

Choose your colours and start painting. Do not think about what you WANT to paint, just trust what comes out on the paper. Go with the flow and continue until you feel that the painting is finished

Step 4:

Sit and take the time to look at the painting. Give it a title. Do not think too much about the name, do it as quick as possible. Write what comes to you. Note how you felt as you painted, and how you feel as you look at the outcome and your experience throughout the process as you painted.

Step 5:

Sign and date the painting.

Materials needed:

Paper; preferably 64 X 90 cm 250GSM

Wallpaper paste if you are using your hands

No need to use paste if you are using brushes

Paintbrushes; any size small medium and large

Poster Paints; White, black, red, blue and yellow (primary colours) or any colours of your choice

A palette for your paints- you can use an old plate

Masking tape

Old rags or paper towels

2 Containers/jars for water

Plastic to protect wall and floor

Soap to clean the brushes after use.

Painting Process:

It is best to place the paper up on a wall, door or window pane. Having the paper at eye level allows you to look up at the paper as you paint. You can be more intuitive when you are looking up while painting rather than having the paper on a table. It will still work rather well, but I find it works better when the paper is upright rather than flat. It is a preference for me.

Standing while you paint allows a freedom of movement with no restrictions. When you use paste, it is best to place a full strip of masking tape on the top of the paper and a small strip on each of the corners at the end. You can also paint while sitting.

Use the paint neat or for lighter effects water it down to the consistency that you want. There is no right or wrong way. Whatever feels right, is right. Go with your intuition.

Before you paint, it is really important to get the paper up and ready so that you do not have to think about what is needed to get started. Have all your materials, brushes, water, paste etc, all laid out and ready, as it is easier to go straight from the meditation to the painting.

Relaxation/Meditation Process

If you are not familiar with meditating, read the following once or twice to get started. Sit and close your eyes. Remember what you have read and allow your body to follow your thoughts:

As you sit in a comfortable position, feel your feet in contact with the floor. Notice how your back is supported and you feel even more secure. Feel your shoulders release and relax even more. With every breath you take, you allow your body to go deeper into a more relaxed state.

Feel your body sink deeper and go softer as you breathe more deeply and easily. Imagine roots growing out and down from the soles of your feet, as they reach outwards and downwards deeper into the floor. The more you allow these roots to grow the more secure and relaxed your body becomes, as your breathing becomes steadier and easier.

Begin the process of allowing yourself to sink into a more relaxed and even deeper state of calmness. Feel this serenity and tranquility wash over you like running warm water as it washes down into the roots and allows them to grow deeper and stronger beneath your feet.

You begin to transcend to a new level of peace and contentment which fills your entire body. Stay in touch with these feelings and emotions and breathe them deeper still, into every single cell and every single organ in our body, from the tip of your toes to the top of your head.

Keep these feelings coursing through your body as you connect and visualise a lighting flame just above the crown of your head, which cleanses you from the inside out. Continue for five to ten minutes minimum. Open your eyes and start to paint.

Conclusion

Heart Art 'Magic' is for, anyone who would like to make a positive change in their life. If there is something that you are not happy with, or more importantly, if you are not happy within yourself, then this book can help to direct you towards the change that is right for you.

You are the only person who knows what change needs to happen in your life. You may not know it at a 'conscious' level, but your 'subconscious' knows what it is, and your internal 'voice' has been trying to give you messages about the changes that could benefit you, but maybe you didn't understand, or you may not have 'listened' to this advice. Or maybe you did understand, and did listen, but have yet to ACT upon the information you were given.

You know when your 'gut feeling' is telling you to be 'aware' of what you are about to do, but you just go ahead and do it anyway. And afterwards you can say to yourself. "I knew I shouldn't have done that, or eaten that" because your body will 'react' in a certain way, letting you know that the decision you made was the wrong one. Why wait until it is too late, when you can choose a positive way of making the right choices for you.

You are an incredible 'human being' in all that you do, yet sometimes, you are so 'tuned out' of how you 'feel' that you stumble through life and 'make do' with whatever life throws your way. When you 'know' what you want in life, you take the logical steps towards 'achieving' it. You definitely would not 'take', or 'make do' with anything less than what you set out to achieve in the first place. Yet you do this to yourself regularly, because you are unclear, as to what it is, that is making you 'feel' drained about certain aspects in your life.

Why is it that there are days you feel drained and other days you feel energised? You can have great days where you feel great and some days you feel you are just not up to the job in hand. When you are doing something you love or have an interest in, this can energise you because it makes you feel good. When we do things that we really do not like, this also has an effect on how we feel and it can drain your energy. The law of 'cause and effect' is at play. For every action, there is an equal and opposite reaction.

Do you know what you want to achieve? Unless you know what that is, there is no way that you can be successful. Start with the things in your life that you do not like or want. This can be your starting point. What areas of your life are you struggling with? Make your list and prioritise from one to ten. What is the first thing on that list that you would like to change?

Then write Who, What, Where. When and Why and How? Apply this strategy to every item on your list, but start with the primary one first. Who and Why?

Who: needs to change?

What: needs to change?

Where: will that change take place?

When: will that change take place?

Why: does it need to change?

How are you going to change it?

A man of knowledge lives by acting, not thinking about acting. *Carlos Casteneda*

Who needs to change?

Rule number one is; the only person that you can change is you. You cannot, and I really mean, you cannot, change anybody else, no matter how hard you try. No matter how much you want to. It is not up to you to change anybody. Everybody has to lead their own life, even if that life is destructive to them. It is their journey, not yours.

Think of that for a few moments. It is liberating to know that you are only responsible for yourself and you need to answer only to yourself for the things that you do in life. As a parent, you are responsible for your children until they become adults and can become responsible for themselves. There is a plan in life for us all, but we need to know what we want, in order for that plan to come to fruition.

Every 'disaster' in your life is not so much a disaster, as a situation waiting for you to change your mind about it. It's not what happens to you in life, it's your perception and it's how you see it, that's important.

Beliefs

The thing always happens that you believe in; and the belief in a thing makes it happen. Frank Lloyd Wright

If you would love to change, then change to love. Loving your self is the best present you can give yourself, and living in the present moment is exhilarating and it can set you free. **Awareness is the key to freedom**. Believe and you can achieve. Make the right choice for yourself; you deserve to be happy, content and empowered.

About the Author

I am a wife and mother of three wonderful children Jennifer, Stephanie and Stephen, who are adults now living their own lives. I am also a very proud grandmother to my two lovely granddaughters Amy aged eight and Keelin, aged four years old. I am very happily married to Damien for over three decades, and I do not know where I would be without his continued love and support, particularly at the times when I needed him most. My entire family stepped in to help me when I could not help myself physically. They had to deal with the running of the household whenever I was unable to do so.

In my Clinic, I practice; Kinesiology, Reflexology, Reiki, Educational Kinesiology, Brain Gym, NLP (Neuro Linguistic Programming), Life Coaching and Heart Art 'Magic' painting process.

Juice Plus+® Personal Franchise provided me with a monthly income when I was physically unable to work in my clinic. I am very proud to be a National Marketing Director and I feel priveliged to help my Juice Plus+® Distributors to become successful.

Nutrition and education play a key role in my practice. You are what you eat. You are what you think. I am available to give the benefit of my experience to any group or individual who would like to hear more on how to make improvements in their health and wellbeing. It can be delivered in person or by skype or webinar.

www.marianegan.ie

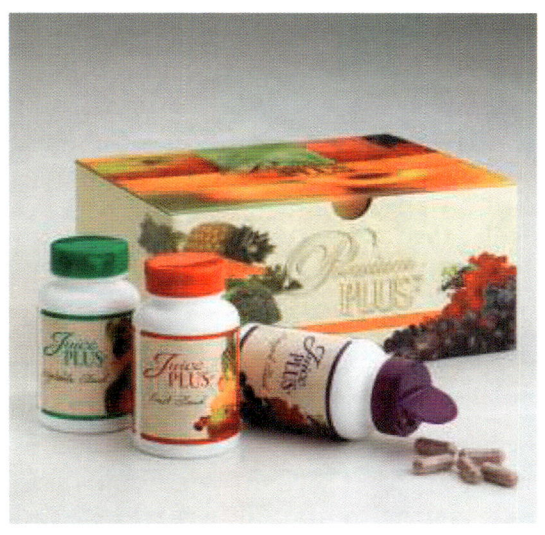

Addendum - My Juice Plus + ® story

I am so grateful for having been introduced to **Juice Plus + ®**

In September 2002, when I got a phone call with an invitation to come to Dublin see a presentation by Dr. Marilyn Joyce, I was undecided as to whether I would or would not go. What made my mind up was the fact that I was visiting my mother that day and I happened to be in Dublin. I was so tired and worn out by the time I got to the hotel that evening that I had decided the best thing for me was to go home and forget about staying for the lecture. I was so uncomfortable in my body and really needed to lie down. I wanted to slide on to the floor and curl up in a ball so that I could get some relief in my body. If I could have done that, I would have, but then I saw a colleague of mine who just arrived and we started talking. As we were catching up Dr. Joyce arrived, so I decided to stay and hear what her presentation was all about.

I listened to what Dr. Joyce had to say and I was blown away by her story of recovery. She is a five times cancer survivor and she shared her story with the audience. When she got her health back she became a published author and she has her owna clinic in the USA. She sees cancer patients and advices them on eating whole **raw** food for prevention. She went through her journey of survival through eating healthy RAW fruit vegetables and berries, which is 'whole live food'. It is the **enzymes** in **raw** food that feeds our cells so that we can remain healthy. Enzymes are what helps us stay healthy and also produces new healthy cells in our body every day.

When we do not get enough of **raw** fruit vegetables and berries, millions of cells die every day and if we are not getting enough of nature's enzymes from food, we cannot replace these cells and we age prematurely.

Juice Plus + ® bridges this gap and provides us with natures nutrition from fresh, **raw**, organic fruit vegetables and berries, which contain the natural enzymes which is the 'life-force' we need. The fruit, vegetables and berries are grown naturally till they reach their peak of ripeness; they are then picked, dried at a very low temperature to preserve the 'life-force' or 'enzyme' activity. The water, sugar and salt are removed and then the powder is packed into capsules. Children can take the capsules as well, but there are little **Juice Plus+®** Soft Chewables for younger children. **Juice Plus + ®** is a great way for those that don't, won't or can't eat **raw** fruit and vegetables every day. Our body can heal itself when it is given the proper nutrition.

I took Dr. Joyce's advice and ordered **Juice Plus+®** that night. It was a great decision. I know I made a wonderful investment in myself. When I heard what she had to say about **Juice Plus+®**, I could not wait to get my hands on them and get the nutrition into my body. I was desperate to get my life back and felt that this was the right choice for me.

My recovery took time, because nature takes time to work. It was a gradual and subtle change that happened over the next few months. **Juice Plus+®** is not a quick fix, it is not a cure for any illness, but for me but it was, and is, a long term solution.

Over time I could feel it working. The longer I was on it the better the results. But it worked, and I was so liberated by the fact that I finally got my physical health back. I became so well that I was able to go back to teaching my fitness classes and I was able to go and open my clinic again. I got my life back. My husband got his wife back and the children got their mother back. It was liberating.

Health is Wealth, and we '**can make a difference**' by eating the foods are body is designed to be nourished by. **Raw**, fruit, vegetables and berries will give your body the energy it needs to function. It is really important to get the proper food to keep us healthy.

If your body is not healthy, where else are you going to live?

To watch the video and for information on **Juice Plus +®** and view the Independent Scientific Studies visit my website.

www.marianegan.ie

The greatest mistake a man can make is to sacrifice health for any other advantage. *Arthur Schopenhauer*

Made in the USA
Charleston, SC
10 May 2011